# CAMBRIDGE
## UNIVERSITY PRESS

University Printing House, Cambridge CB2 8BS, United Kingdom

One Liberty Plaza, 20th Floor, New York, NY 10006, USA

477 Williamstown Road, Port Melbourne, VIC 3207, Australia

314–321, 3rd Floor, Plot 3, Splendor Forum, Jasola District Centre,
New Delhi – 110025, India

103 Penang Road, #05–06/07, Visioncrest Commercial, Singapore 238467

Cambridge University Press is part of the University of Cambridge.

It furthers the University's mission by disseminating knowledge in the pursuit of
education, learning, and research at the highest international levels of excellence.

www.cambridge.org
Information on this title: www.cambridge.org/9781009010566
DOI: 10.1017/9781009023801

First published 2021

A catalogue record for this publication is available from the British Library.

ISBN 978-1-009-01056-6 Paperback
ISSN 2632-332X (online)
ISSN 2632-3311 (print)

Cambridge University Press has no responsibility for the persistence or accuracy of
URLs for external or third-party internet websites referred to in this publication
and does not guarantee that any content on such websites is, or will remain,
accurate or appropriate.

# Cambridge Elements ≡

**Elements in Defence Economics**
edited by
Keith Hartley
*University of York*

# THE US DEFENSE ECONOMY

## Jomana Amara
*Naval Postgraduate School*

## Raymond E. Franck
*USAF Academy*

**CAMBRIDGE**
UNIVERSITY PRESS

# The US Defense Economy

Elements in Defence Economics

DOI: 10.1017/9781009023801
First published online: December 2021

Jomana Amara
*Naval Postgraduate School*

Raymond E. Franck
*USAF Academy*

**Author for correspondence:** Raymond E. Franck, Cfranck215@aol.com

**Abstract:** The US defense economy is remarkable for a number of reasons – including sheer size. It receives a significant (albeit decreasing) share of GDP and has a significant international footprint. Its purpose is to provide the resources for national defense – against a set of complex and capable adversaries. The main players in the defense economy are households and the federal government. The associated interactions determine the resources provided for national defense and their allocation among various defense needs. This Element focuses primarily on interactions between government and industrial suppliers – within the institutional peculiarities of the defense marketplace. This Includes the developments that have determined the course of defense industry consolidation post-Cold War. The authors also highlight the persistent gap between resources available for defense and the means to execute the National Security Strategy. Finally, they offer some tentative thoughts regarding developments likely to shape the defense economy's future.

Keywords: defense economics, US defense economy, US defense industries, US defense industrial consolidation, US defense market regulation

**JEL classifications:** H56, N42, O38

ISBNs: 9781009010566 (PB), 9781009023801 (OC)
ISSNs: 2632-332X (online), 2632-3311 (print)

# Contents

# 1 Introduction

The US defense economy is remarkable for its institutional peculiarities and sheer size. In 2019, with global defense expenditures estimated at $1.9 trillion,[1] US defense expenditures, at around $737 billion, accounted for approximately 39% of the global total (SIPRI, 2020a). The US Department of Defense (DoD) budget dwarfs the budget of the second largest spender, China, estimated at $250 billion for 2018 in 2018 US dollars. China is followed by Saudi Arabia at $68 billion, India at $67 billion, France at $64 billion, and Russia at $61 billion. Even though the DoD budget has been increasing in absolute numbers, it has been decreasing as a percentage of US GDP. Figure 1 illustrates the gradual decline from the Korean war to the present and projects the data to 2025.

The defense economy also has a significant international footprint. The United States is, and has been, the world's leading exporter of defense goods and services; it is also a major arms importer. However, imports are on a much smaller scale, due, inter alia, to strong "Buy American" preferences thoroughly embedded in legislation, policy, and politics. A 2018 US Government Accountability Office (GAO) report estimated that "in fiscal year 2017, foreign end products accounted for less than 5% – about $7.8 billion – of federal obligations for products potentially subject to the Buy American Act" (US Government Accountability Office, 2018, p. 12).

The underlying relationships of a defense economy and its resource allocation are significantly different from those for a textbook market economy. This element will outline the U.S. defense economy and its components. The first section is an overview of the defense economy – identifying the essentials, including the roles of the various players. The second section will address defense resources: to include past experience; the decision-making processes; and the role of the planning, programming, and budgeting process in defense resources allocation. The third section covers the defense marketplace and peculiarities associated with the government's sovereign monopsony. The fourth section regards a rather detailed discussion of defense industrial consolidation post-Cold War – to include assessments of the results. Next (the fifth section) is a discussion of the limits and burdens of a sovereign monopsony. Finally, we consider that the defense economy is a dynamic environment that is driven, inter alia, by rapid changes in defense technology and the state of military affairs.

# 2 Economics of US Defense: An Overview

## 2.1 Major Components of the Defense Economy

The key to understanding the defense economy is knowing the major players and the characteristics that differentiate the defense economy from the general economy.

---

[1] All expenditures converted to US dollars at prevailing exchange rates.

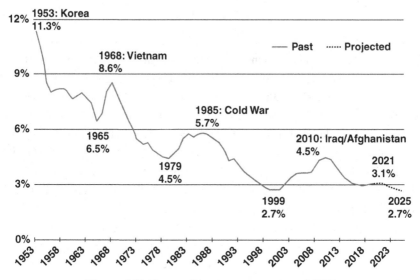

**Figure 1** DoD spending as a percentage of GDP
**Source:** DoD spending as a percentage of GDP compares DoD outlays, both discretionary and "mandatory," from the National Defense Budget Estimates for fiscal year (FY) 2020 (table 7-7) and projected GDP from OMB's Economic Assumptions for the FY 2021 (Office of the Under Secretary of Defense, 2020a)

However, the boundary between the defense and nondefense sectors is fuzzy at best. For example, the military forces have both the active and reserve components. To what extent are reservists a part of the defense establishment and defense economy or the general economy?[2] Employment in defense industries is even more difficult to estimate. Some firms sell only commercial products to both defense and commercial customers. Most firms that are clearly in the defense economy nonetheless also have commercial sales. This lack of clear demarcation is indicated in the wide range of estimates for defense industry employment (e.g., Hartley, 2017, esp. p. 33), which appears in Table 1.

With that reservation in mind, Figure 2 depicts the basic structure and flows of the defense economy. The main players are households that provide resources to support national defense (a public good); the federal government – executive, legislative, and judicial branches (the purchasing agent); and the Defense Industrial Base (DIB; the defense firms who also do business in the international market). The interactions between the players determine the resources raised for national defense and their allocation among defense needs.

---

[2] The best answer seems "both," but raises the question of how these individuals "split" their economic identities.

**Table 1** Estimates of defense industry employment. All numbers are in thousands

| Data source (year) | Defense industrial | Commercial aerospace | Total direct | Indirect employment | Total employment |
|---|---|---|---|---|---|
| AIA (2018) | 355 | 488 | 843 | 1,587 | 2,430 |
| Deloitte (2016) | 845 | 331 | 1,233 | 2,909 | 4,141 |

**Sources:** AIA (2018, esp. p. 1); Deloitte (2016, esp. p. 5)

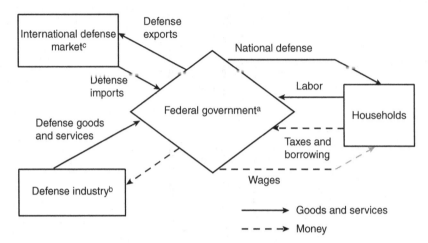

**Figure 2** Flow diagram of the defense economy
**Notes:** [a] The federal government provides national defense (a public good) to its citizens (the "households"). To do this, it collects taxes from the households (and incurs debt on their behalf). It also hires, and pays, a defense work force – military and civilian. The government also purchases commercial goods and services (e.g., office supplies) from the general economy. [b] A sector of the economy (defense industry) supplies defense-specific goods (e.g., warplanes) and services (e.g., research activities). [c] The government also participates in the international defense market. It imports defense goods and services, and, since government controls military exports, it is the international sales agent for the defense industry.

However, a significant part of the defense market is for defense-specific goods. The federal government is the sole customer of most defense-specific goods and services, and makes the rules for how that market operates. Additionally, defense goods and services are generally produced to a government-determined set of specifications or "requirements," for which the government pays development costs.

As the sole customer[3] (monopsonist) for defense-specific goods and services, the federal government is also a sovereign monopsonist,[4] defining market

---

[3] Even though the United States exports military goods and services, the US government is nonetheless the most significant and, in many cases, the only customer. For specialized defense products, the US government almost always defines the product and pays for development costs. The defense products may be made available for export. Also, the government can veto virtually any arms sale abroad – through its various arms export authorities (discussed later on in the context of the export control regime).

[4] A good alternate term for "sovereign monopolist" is "customer, sponsor and regulator" (Heidenkamp *et al.*, 2013).

structures, rules, and norms. Accordingly, any discussion of the US defense marketplace must pay attention to rules and policies, and their effects. Figure 2 demonstrates the central position of the federal government, necessitating the need to understand government players, institutions, and processes. A rather lengthy and complicated set of processes starts with assessment of defense needs and translation of needs to defense resources. Basically, the Executive Branch, through the Planning, Programming, Budgeting, and Execution System (PPBES), starts with a strategy and ends with the President's Budget (PB) submitted to Congress. The Congress receives the PB, and proceeds to formulate authorization and appropriations bills for national defense in the coming fiscal year. The judiciary resolves disputes. In particular, the courts have been involved in bid-protest litigation.

But there is another set of players not included in Figure 2 that are involved in the defense economy. These are the organizations that analyze defense policy and resource questions – and contribute to ongoing policy deliberations. The following are offered as representative examples.

### 2.1.1 Agencies within the Executive and Legislative Branches

- Executive
  - Organic to the services or reporting to the Secretary of Defense
    - Cost Analysis and Program Evaluation (CAPE)
    - studies and analysis groups within service staffs
    - research arms of various military educational institutions like the Naval Postgraduate School

  - Organizations closely affiliated with the services or DoD
    - the RAND Corporation
    - Institute for Defense Analysis
    - Center for Naval Analysis

- Legislative
  - Congressional Budget Office (CBO), Congressional Research Service, and GAO.

- "Think tanks," such as the Lexington Institute, with ties to defense industrial firms; and independent organizations such as the Brookings Institution, American Enterprise Institute, Hudson Institute, Heritage Foundation, Federation of American Scientists, Center for Strategic and Budgetary Analysis, and Center for a New American Security

- A number of periodicals such as *Air Force Magazine*, *Naval Institute Proceedings*, *Marine Corps Gazette*, *ARMY Magazine*, *National Interest*, and *National Defense*.

These "auxiliary" participants in the defense economy are well represented in our list of sources.

## 2.2 Goals of the Defense Economy

The defense economy provides the material means for "national defense," which immediately begs two questions: (1) against what threat or threats, and (2) how much defense is actually provided with the resources committed? Hitch *et al.* (1960) answered the first question primarily with come-as-you-are contingencies: nuclear confrontation and conventional warfare at various levels of intensity (pp. 11–14). Their answer to the second question depends on the following (Hitch *et al.*, 1960, pp. 3–4):

- How much is available for defense?
- How much of what is available is allocated to defense?
- How well are those resources used?

For how much is available, Hitch *et al.* (1960) cited the size of GDP, present and future (pp. 28–40). How much is allocated belongs generally in the realm of politics, broadly defined. How well the resources are used concerns efficiency of resource use, the major theme of their work (see esp. pp. 1–14). Moreover, the allocation of defense resources can be a question of governmental politics as much as resource allocation as economists generally understand it.

One major goal of Hitch *et al.* (1960) was to provide a better framework for defense resource allocation – oriented toward programs and associated capabilities rather than objects like military hardware (pp. 49–51). The result was a system of programs organized in a hierarchy of resource packages. This system, changed somewhat, is still the heart of DoD resource allocation.

During the Cold War, the major threat was the Soviet Union, with some lesser contingencies added. Life has since become much more complicated. US defense planning must now account for a large number and variety of threats and adversaries. These include peer or near-peer rivals such as China and Russia, nuclear-armed smaller powers primarily North Korea and Iran, and a constantly changing and evolving set of insurgent movements, such as Al Qaeda and ISIS, and other non-state actors like Hezbollah and narcotics cartels.[5] They are generally well-resourced, imaginative, resilient, and adaptable.

---

[5] In our opinion, the best one-volume discussion of these threats appears in *The Dragons and the Snakes* (Kilcullen, 2020).

# 3 Resources for Defense

## 3.1 Past Allocations to National Defense

While a larger economy has more resources available, *ceteris paribus*, there are other relevant considerations. As Hitch *et al.* (1960) point out, resources for defense carry an opportunity cost in other public needs foregone (e.g., p. 4). How much of GDP is available in the twenty-first century for federal government purposes? A practical answer appears to be 20%+, in "normal" times.

The federal portion of GDP is likely to change slowly over the next decade – with the COVID-19 recession being a wild card. What has also happened is that the "human resources" portion of the federal budget has increased steadily and significantly. At the same time, the defense share of GDP (and fraction of federal expenditures) has decreased. In the mid-1950s, defense accounted for about 10% of GDP, and is now about 3.5%. So, while resources for defense increase in response to assessed threats, resources for defense, as a fraction of GDP, have steadily decreased in the long run – as shown in Figure 3.

Furthermore, it is reasonable to expect that the portion of GDP available for defense will continue to decline for the foreseeable future. The human resources portion of the federal budget will continue to increase with an aging population. Of course, the COVID-19 epidemic, with its expensive mitigation programs, will increase national debt and debt service as a fraction of GDP, with further pressure on "discretionary" categories like defense.

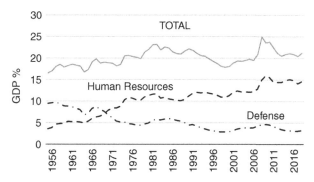

**Figure 3** Federal outlays by category (1956–2020)
**Note:** In US Office of Management and Budget parlance, "human resources" is a budget superfunction. The constituent functions are education, training, employment, and social services; health; Medicare; income security; social security; and "various benefits and services."
**Source:** US Office of Management and Budget (2020) FY 2021

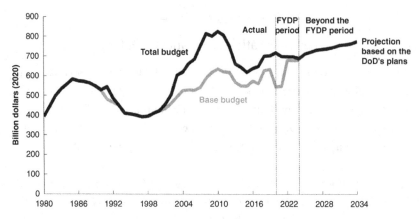

**Figure 4** National defense real outlays

Post-2001, DoD funding is divided into base and non-base funding. Base funding supports daily military and civilian operations and includes the development and procurement of systems – basically all normal peacetime activities

**Note:** FYDP, Future Years Defense Program

**Source:** Congressional Budget Office (2019); US Office of Management and Budget (2020)

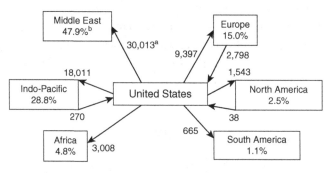

**Figure 5** US arms trade by region (2014–2019)

**Notes:** Regions per US DoD combatant command areas of responsibility. [a] Millions of SIPRI TIVs (trend indicator values). TIV is an SIPRI arms export measure, which assigns "values" for different categories of military goods. It is intended to better measure the military implications of any transfer, rather than financial value of transactions (SIPRI, 2020c, section 2). [b] Percentage of total exports.

**Source:** SIPRI (2020b)

Between 2019 and 2030, federal expenditures are expected to increase from 20 to 23% of GDP; but growth in the percentages for mandatory programs and net interest payments reduce the discretionary portion of federal spending to 5.8%, with 2.9% going to defense in 2030 versus 3.5% in 2020 (Congressional Budget Office, 2020).

## 3.2 The Defense Economy's Footprint

The US defense economy depends for the most part on government expenditures. Figure 4 shows real defense expenditures from 1980 to 2034. One can observe four "eras." First was the later Cold War in the 1980s. Second was a post-Cold War decline with an associated "procurement holiday" in the 1990s. With a lot of new equipment in hand from the 1980s buildup, the natural place to cut spending was in procurement (Wayne, 1998a) (see also Figure 6). The third featured various contingency operations following the World Trade Center attacks in 2001; and fourth, the Budget Control Act of 2011.

In the post 2001 era, the Total Obligation Authority (TOA) included annual allowances for Overseas Contingency Operations (OCOs) over and above the "base" DoD budget. The difference between the upper and lower line in Figure 4, the base budget, reflects this.

The base budget appropriations categories are:

○ military personnel, which covers pay, cash benefits, costs of retirement benefits, and the military health system for military personnel and retirees (Figure 7);
○ operation and maintenance, which includes the pay, cash benefits, costs of retirement benefits for civilian employees of DoD, and costs such as fuel, base maintenance and operations, and spare parts;
○ procurement, research, development, test, and evaluation (RDT&E), which is used to develop and purchase new systems, to upgrade existing systems, and develop future systems (Figure 8);
○ military construction;

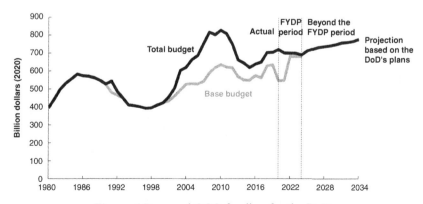

**Figure 6** Base and OCO funding for the DoD

**Note:** FYDP, Future Years Defense Program

**Source:** Congressional Budget Office (2019)

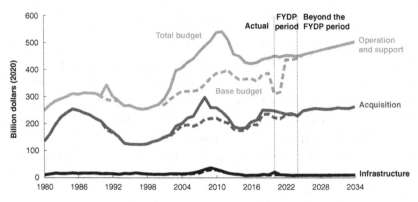

**Figure 7** Funding for the DoD: Acquisition and operations
**Source:** Congressional Budget Office (2019)

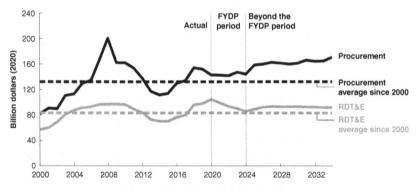

**Figure 8** DoD acquisition funding
**Source:** Congressional Budget Office (2019)

- family housing;
- revolving and management funds (Congressional Budget Office, 2019).[6]

The costs for military personnel and operations and maintenance constitute approximately two-thirds of the DoD's total budget request.

Non-base funding is referred to as OCO funding and is considered a form of emergency funding for what are intended to be temporary activities, such as the wars in Afghanistan and Iraq. Figure 4 details the base and OCO funding for the DoD. The difference on the graph between the total budget and the base budget represents OCO funding.

---

[6] Revolving funds are established to finance a continuing cycle of business operations. Revolving fund accounts are authorized to be credited with receipts, incur obligations, and make expenditures. Fund collections are normally available for obligation and expenditure without further action by the Congress.

However, only about 15% of OCO funding requested by the DoD for 2020 and 2021 directly supported actual offshore operations. The overwhelming bulk of the OCO funding for these two years (about 85%) supports the base budget in order to avoid the spending limits imposed under the Budget Control Act of 2011. Even though the caps were increased in the Bipartisan Budget Act in 2019, the increases were not sufficient to cover the base expenses in 2020 and 2021. The OCO funding projected on the graph from 2022 to 2025 is intended as a placeholder and reflects the difficulty and uncertainty in forecasting future overseas operations (Congressional Budget Office, 2019).[7]

## 3.3 Participation in the Global Arms Trade

The United States is also a major international arms trader for both exports and imports. It is the largest arms exporter by far, but also a significant importer, ranked 15th worldwide (SIPRI, 2020b). However, imports have been relatively small. The US DoD purchases almost all of its needs domestically due to the US defense industry's competence and the Buy American Act. The original legislation dates to 1933. The Berry Amendment of 1941 requires 100% US content for a number of products, such as textiles, clothing, and footwear (Platzer, 2020). In addition, DoD has a mandate to penalize non-US content in acquisition proposals by increasing the bid's evaluated cost (Gallacher, 2019). In FY 2017, DoD purchased about 4%, $7.8 billion, of its end items valued at $196 billion from foreign sources. Those foreign purchases were usually due to various exceptions and waivers, such as use abroad, trade agreement waiver, exception for DoD qualifying country of origin (US Government Accountability Office, 2018, summarized in the highlights).

## 3.4 Defense Resources versus Defense Needs: "If It Ain't Funded, It Ain't"[8]

### *3.4.1 Near-Term Fiscal Constraints*

As noted previously, long-term prospects for supporting the current National Security Strategy are problematic (Edelman *et al.*, 2018) and near-term funding prospects also appear dim. While current threats and technical opportunities are numerous, current resources are decidedly constrained. The military establishment entered the 2020s with forces lacking the size and composition to fully meet the demands of the current security environment. For example, the Navy

---

[7] The US government fiscal year runs from October 1 to September 30 (Congressional Budget Office, 2019).

[8] An old saying in the Pentagon.

has a long-term goal of 382–466 battle force ships, plus large, unmanned vessels. The current force size is 297 (O'Rourke, 2021, p. 2).

The Navy also proposes a more distributed fleet architecture to counter evolving threats (O'Rourke, 2021, pp. 9, 21). The need to change force composition to address critical planning contingencies is recognized throughout the DoD. The Marine Corps is a particularly good case in point (Feickert, 2021; Mizokami, 2021). In short, the services need to modernize, restructure, and get larger.

To complicate the problem, the DoD has a significant readiness and support deficit. Examples include:

- The B-1B heavy bomber developed a number of readiness problems, associated with operations in Iraq and Afghanistan. Those have been addressed, but at a cost (Tirpak, 2020).
- The Navy's combat ships periodic maintenance needs exceed the capacity of current shipyards, due in large part to shortfalls in both physical and human capital (US Government Accountability Office, 2020, esp. fig. 6, p. 14).
- The Air Force has abandoned efforts to achieve the DOD's 80%, mission-capable goal (Insinna and Losey, 2020).

There is indeed good evidence that the DoD does not have the resources to pay for those larger, restructured, and more modern forces (Congressional Research Service, 2020c, pp. 4–5, 33; Judson, 2020; Wood, 2018). The COVID-19 situation and aftermath potentially worsens the situation (e.g., Congressional Budget Office, 2021).

Also, the DoD operates part of most fiscal years with continuing resolutions in lieu of a budget with appropriated funds (Hallman, 2019). The effect has been, among other things, to delay programs and new initiatives that both the Executive and Legislative branches agree are appropriate (McCusker, 2020). These inefficiencies are largely a result of a separation-of-powers governmental structure. But the effects are nonetheless real – particularly in relatively austere fiscal environments.

Among other things, the DoD will also have to make tough resource allocation decisions in the near future. These include current versus future capabilities (e.g., Eaglen, 2020; Spoehr, 2020); conventional versus nuclear modernization (Weisgerber, 2020); and an intensified quarrel over the services' shares of the budget (Harper, 2020).

### 3.4.2 Fiscal Constraints: Future

Sustained real growth for defense budgets is easy to advocate say but difficult to implement in current economic and budgetary conditions. In fact, it seems a practical impossibility within the CBO's current base case. With expected

COVID-19 economic disruptions, the CBO base case includes real GDP growth of about 1.6% per year between 2019 and 2030 (Shackleton, 2020, p. 3). However, growth in entitlement programs increases mandatory spending to 15.3% of GDP in 2030, versus 13.5% in 2019. Also, net interest increases as a share of GDP, 1.6–2.2%, due to continued deficits and interest rate increases from the 2020s very low levels (Congressional Budget Office, 2020, p. 19). In addition, the base case includes federal revenues remaining at about 18% of GDP (Congressional Budget Office, 2020, p. 18).

The US response to the new threat environment has been captured in the National Security Strategy of 2017 and succeeding documents (The White House, 2017). The capabilities to execute the national strategy are contained in the National Defense Strategy of 2018 (US Department of Defense, 2018a). In the current planning environment, the associated resources involve an extended 3–5% increase in the real defense budget. This assessment comes from a previous Secretary of Defense and a Congressionally mandated study (Edelman *et al.*, 2018, p. 52): "We believe that three to five percent annual real growth is indicative of the investment required. Failing that, it may be necessary to alter the expectations of US defense strategy and our global strategic objectives."

## 3.5 Department of Defense Budget Processes

Annually, the civilian and military leadership in the DoD uses the Planning, Programming, Budgeting, and Execution framework for allocating resources based on their strategic objectives. As defined in the DoD's directive 7045.14, PPBE is intended to "provide the DOD with the most effective mix of forces, equipment, manpower, and support attainable within fiscal constraints" (McGarry, 2020). The PPBE cycle anticipates the year of budget execution by two years and produces a budget that the President submits to Congress.

The planning phase of PPBE is led by the Under Secretary of Defense for Policy and results in the Defense Planning Guidance (DPG), produced with guidance from the various strategy documents such as the National Security Strategy, National Defense Strategy, and National Military Strategy. This ensures that the DPG details force development priorities that align with the current Administration's vision and goals.

The aim of the programming phase of PPBE is to consider the future force that results from present resource decisions. The programming phase results in a Program Objective Memorandum (POM) developed by each military service and agency and guided by the DPG. The POM proposes resource requirements, forces, manpower, and funding for the coming five years and serves as an input and update into the Future Years Defense Program (FYDP). The FYDP is a forecast of resources required for the DoD and is typically generated every year during the programming phase of PPBE.

In the budgeting phase, the military services submit a budget estimate, reviewed by the DoD Comptroller, for the FYDP. The Comptroller office ensures that the service requests align with the overall DoD budget. The service requests are then input into the final funding request presented to Congress by the President. The FYDP is updated to reflect the DoD's final request and links the DoD's resource inputs to its outputs and groups funding by programs instead of activities (McGarry, 2020).

Execution is the final phase of the PBBE process. The intent of this phase is to evaluate program results – how well a program actually performs in comparison to its planned performance. Execution review occurs concurrently with program and budget review.

The FYDP, generated and finalized in the programming and budgeting phases respectively of PPBE, is a five-year plan for the budget that requests funding for the upcoming year and discloses the planned budgets under ordinary operations for the next four years (McGarry and Peters, 2020). It is submitted to Congress as part of the President's budget request. The FYDP outlines the resources, both material and manpower, required to support DoD programs. For example, the 2020 FYDP consists of the request for 2020 funding and the budgets planned for 2021–2024. The 2020 FYDP will also outline the two previous fiscal years' appropriations.

The FYDP can be considered a database linking inputs/resources to outputs/ programs. It presents three types of information: total obligatory authority, which are the appropriated funds; manpower, both military and civilian; and forces, both equipment and combat units. The FYDP outputs are grouped into twelve major forces programs, with each program enumerating the three inputs or resources dedicated to the program. Six of the programs are combat force programs: strategic forces; general purpose forces; command, control, communications, intelligence, and space; mobility forces; guard and reserve forces; and special operations. The remaining six programs are support programs: research and development; central supply and maintenance; training, medical, and other personnel activities; administration and associated activities; support of other nations; and national security space.[9]

The graph categories in Figure 7 are generated by CBO and used in their analyses. Operations and support are the sum of military personnel

---

[9] A major force program for national security space, Program 12 (MFP-12), was created in response to congressional direction in the FY 2016 National Defense Authorization Act and helped keep track of the space activities of the DoD.

appropriations, operations and maintenance, and revolving and management funds. Acquisition funding includes appropriations for procurement and funds for RDT&E. Military construction and family housing are the two components of infrastructure appropriations.

The graph categories in Figure 8 are likewise generated by CBO. Acquisition funding includes the funding for procurement and RDT&E.

## 3.6 Resources: Department of Defense Manpower[10]

As of July 30, 2020, the total number of active personnel in the US military was 1,382,922, with 481,939 in the Army; 342,161 in the Navy; 182,658 in the Marine Corps; 334,135 in the Air Force; and 42,029 in the Coast Guard. The National Guard and Reserve support the DoD in various functions and number around 800,000 between the Army, Navy, Marine Corps, Air, National Guard and Reserve, and Coast Guard Reserve. In addition to active duty personnel, the DoD employs around 760,000 civilians (Defense Manpower Data Center, 2020). The total number of personnel supporting the DoD in some capacity is approximately 3 million – this makes the DoD the largest employer in the world, with Walmart in second place at about 2.2 million employees.

### 3.6.1 Cost of Manpower

The single largest expense category for the DoD is the cost of manpower, both military and civilian, estimated at about $281 billion in 2020, approximately 40% of the budget.[11] Military pay and benefits that include health care, military housing, schools for DoD dependents, commissaries, incentive pay, childcare, and other military family support programs constitute approximately a third of the DoD's budget. The military health care system, which provides medical care for military personnel and retirees, totaling $51.4 billion in 2020, is a rapidly growing expense for the DoD (Office of the Under Secretary of Defense, 2020b). The CBO predicts that the costs of compensation of military personnel will continue to grow at higher rates than inflation (Congressional Budget Office, 2019). Personnel costs are spread over several budget categories: military personnel, which covers pay, cash benefits, costs of retirement benefits, and the military health care system for military personnel and retirees; operation and maintenance, which includes the pay, cash benefits, and costs of retirement

---

[10] The information in this Section, unless otherwise noted, comes primarily from Amara (2019).

[11] The authors' calculations for the cost of manpower includes military compensation, TRICARE for life accrual payments, civilian compensation, and the military health care system. The DoD budget used in the calculation is the total budget including the base and non-base budget – $718 billion. Calculations are based on figures reported in the Congressional Budget Office (2019).

benefits for civilian employees of DoD; and family housing (Congressional Budget Office, 2019).

### 3.6.2 Costs of an All-Volunteer Force

To understand personnel costs as the single largest expense for the DoD, we need to understand the budgetary and economic costs of the all-volunteer force. The US military relied for most of its history on an all-volunteer force. However, at the commencement of the Korean war in 1950, which also marked the start of the Cold War, the United States instituted the draft without a major war in progress. Public opinion in the United States turned against the draft in the late 1960s and early 1970s during the Vietnam war's escalation. In addition, the draft was perceived as arbitrary and unfair due to the many exemption conditions and deferrals. For example, in 1962, because of low demand for conscripts, the US military only called about 4% of the 1.8 million draft eligible men. The remaining 96% were deferred because of educational, occupational, and paternity reasons. Eventually, the deferments were also extended to married men. In fact, conscripts constituted less than 50% of enlisted personnel. The remaining volunteered. Ultimately, economic reasoning and cost and benefit analysis of conscription played a crucial role in ending the draft. In 1969, President Nixon established a commission to end the draft and transform the military to an all-volunteer force. The commission stated that the nation's interests are best served by moving to an all-volunteer force. The commission also recommended offering incentives to increase the appeal of a military career and attract high-quality personnel. The incentives included items such as recruitment bonuses and increased military pay to compete with the civilian sector for talent.

The cost of moving to an all-volunteer force versus that of a conscript force became a major consideration in the commission's deliberations. Advocates for the status quo argued that the cost of a conscript force is less than that of an all-volunteer force because of the higher compensation for volunteers. However, the advocates for an all-volunteer force argued successfully that in addition to budget costs, which are higher for an all-volunteer force, the total cost of economic resources used by the forces has to be considered. The economic costs include opportunity cost, cost of evading service, recruiting costs, and economic loss associated with higher taxation levels.

Opportunity cost is the value forgone when an individual gives up a civilian career to join the military. The costs include lost civilian wages, civilian sector goods that are not produced, and the intangible costs of giving up civilian life and career for a military one. Economic theory holds that individuals will join the military when the military's compensation exceeds the individual's opportunity cost of civilian life. In a conscription system that randomly selects recruits, the opportunity cost of conscription will always be higher than an all-volunteer force.

Thus, compensation costs for military personnel, which consist of pay and cash benefits for military personnel and the DoD's civilian employees, the costs of retirement benefits, housing allowances, and subsistence allowances, have risen rapidly over time to where the CBO predicts that the costs of compensation for military personnel will continue to increase at historical rates, growing faster than inflation. The CBO projects that the costs will increase at an average annual rate of one percentage point above economywide inflation if Congress and the President continue the current personnel policies (Congressional Budget Office, 2019).

Hence, the budgetary costs involved in paying compensation to an all-volunteer force are higher than those for a conscript force, resulting in a higher level of taxation on the public. However, depending on the cost of technology used as a force multiplier that can only be effectively used by a professional force, the full budgetary costs of the volunteer force could conceivably be lower or higher than that of a conscript force. Additionally, the nation incurs economic losses from distortions in the behavior of business and individuals in response to tax increases. The distortions are proportional to the military compensation costs. Compensation levels rise exponentially with an all-volunteer force, linearly for a conscript force. Thus, the distortion tends to rise significantly with the expansion of the volunteer force.

The government expends resources to prevent individuals from evading the draft. This cost is nonexistent in an all-volunteer force and can be quite high for a conscript force during unpopular times to serve or when civil society is not highly supportive of the military. The costs of evasion fall on both the government and the individual. The individual expends effort and cost to avoid the draft when the benefits from evasion are higher than the costs of serving. The government expends resources to decrease avoidance of service in order to maintain credibility. The cost of evading service is no longer a cost that is relevant.

The approach to recruiting, training, and retention is quite different between a draft and volunteer force. Resources and budgetary costs for recruitment are almost nonexistent for a conscript force and consist of tests to identify unqualified personnel. However, the volunteer force requires a sustained and successful recruiting campaign to inform and attract highly functional recruits to join, at the same time, retention rates and length of service tend to be higher. Due to the high turnover and constant retraining, training costs tend to be higher for a draft force.

## 3.7 Diversity

The socioeconomic, racial, and ethnic makeup of the US military is highly representative of the population, with some exceptions such as geographic distribution: the South is more heavily represented. This could result from attitudes to the military, since the South is the only region where over half, approximately 53%, of the population surveyed would recommend the military as a career. While the Northeast is somewhat underrepresented, the remaining regions are roughly evenly represented.[12] Active-duty military personnel are younger than the general population. Military personnel between the ages of 17 and 24 constitute 49% of the force in comparison to the civilian workforce at 19%. The military typically prefers a younger force and constructs its policies to encourage a younger makeup of recruits. By law, recruits must be between 17 and 42 years old and personnel rarely serve more than 30 years. These policies intentionally produce an active-duty population younger than the overall civilian sector.

## 3.8 Gender

Prior to 1967, the US military restricted the percentage of female personnel to 2% of the forces. After the move to a volunteer force, the role of women in the forces expanded and women are increasingly serving in combat-arms professions that were previously off limits to them. Until recently, women were barred from ground combat operations, from certain units such as special forces, and from Navy submarines. However, women are still underrepresented and constitute 15% of active-duty personnel while making up approximately 50% of the working-age population.[13]

A main concern when conscription ended in the United States was that recruits from the lowest socioeconomic background, with limited economic opportunity, would join in numbers higher than their representation in the general population and that children of families in the middle- and upper-income households would choose alternate careers. While the data are imperfect and conclusions should be

---

[12] We use the US Census Bureau's definition of regions. The Northeast contains Maine, New Hampshire, Vermont, Massachusetts, Rhode Island, Connecticut, New York, New Jersey, and Pennsylvania. The South covers Delaware, Maryland, the District of Columbia, Virginia, West Virginia, North Carolina, South Carolina, Georgia, Florida, Kentucky, Tennessee, Alabama, Mississippi, Arkansas, Louisiana, Oklahoma, and Texas.

[13] The low levels of women's representation in the DoD could stem from many different factors, such as the supply of interested applicants, recruiting policies, and rates of retention.

taken tentatively, the consensus of the research indicates that the majority of enlisted recruits came from middle- or lower-middle-income families – potentially as much as 60%. Although, the military is less likely to see recruits from the highest and lowest income households, it has successfully attracted some young people from these two groups.

The composition of the active-duty enlisted members of the armed forces is largely racially and ethnically diverse and closely mirrors the general population. Minority personnel constituted 26% of the enlisted forces and 14% of commissioned officers.

African Americans are the largest minority group, constituting of 13–19% of enlisted personnel at various times. The African American community is about 14% of the general population. Hispanics constitute about 11% of the enlisted forces, which is lower than their percentage in the general population at 14%. Other racial groups such as Asians, Native Americans, and Pacific Islanders make up 7% of enlisted personnel, close to the 6% that they represent in the general population. The racial and ethnic composition is different for the officer corps, with 8% of newly commissioned officers being African Americans and 4% Hispanic. These percentages closely match the proportion of these groups in similar college-educated civilian populations. Other racial groups such as Asians, Native Americans, and Pacific Islanders make up 5% of the officer corps, which is close to their 6% makeup of similar groups in the general population.

## 3.9 Employment in Defense Industries

Since there is no clear and unambiguous standard definition of what constitutes defense industrial employment, estimating the number of people employed in defense industries is difficult. Researchers making inquiries into defense employment and particularly those making international comparisons are likely to encounter serious data issues due to multiple definitions of defense employment. For example, defense employment could be defined as working in end-item production, or working with lower-tier suppliers to primary producers of defense material and being potentially unaware of the connections with a defense firm. Various US defense industrial employment estimates range from a low of 800,000 to a high of 3,500,000. Aeronautical Industries Association (AIA) and Deloitte, a global consulting company actively involved in the defense sector, have estimated defense employment using two different methodologies. Table 1 summarizes the estimates.

AIA developed a methodology with IHS Markit using some proprietary information. The remaining data came from sources such as the Census Bureau, Bureau of Labor Statistics, and from the American Association for the Advancement of Science. Deloitte then estimates direct employment for specified North American Industry Classification System (NAICS) codes from Bureau of Labor Statistics data in addition to various corporate reports. Deloitte them estimates connections with other codes using the Bureau of Economic Analysis's Regional Input-Output Modeling System.

While both the AIA and Deloitte methodologies are credible, they involve methods and data not fully disclosed, making these estimates impossible to replicate and verify. Furthermore, the reported results vary significantly, which likely results from the variance in the underlying methods.

Basically, "employment" in the defense economy is difficult to define, because, *inter alia,* "defense industry" is difficult to define. As Hartley (2017) states: "National governments often do not provide official statistics on their defense industries, usually because of the difficulties of defining them" (p. 32).

## 4 The Defense Market: A Sovereign Monopsony

As noted, a significant portion of defense expenditures involve highly specialized goods and services – particularly in the investment accounts. Most of DoD investment is RDT&E and procurement, which is used to develop those highly specialized items.

## 4.1 Research, Development, Technology, and Evaluation

A wide range of issues such as current military engagements, international commitments, near-term national security threats, the need for developing technological capabilities to tackle emerging and unexpected threats, funding levels of adversaries and allies, and prior commitments inform Congress's decision about funding levels for DoD RDT&E (Sargent, 2020, pp. 10–20).

The DoD develops its research and technology by funding industry, universities, and federal and other laboratories. It also increasingly relies on transfer of technology developed by the private sector for commercial use. The DoD faces a series of challenges to its RDT&E programs. These include a changing mindset away from federal government funding research; an increased role of commercial companies developing technology that is available to all; increased competition in technology development from non-US companies; and an erratic level of funding available for research (Wong *et al.*, 1998).

The DoD, in FY 2020, spent approximately $108.6 billion on RDT&E, 41.4% of all federal research appropriations and 58% more than the next largest recipient, the Department of Health and Human Services. Approximately 97%

of DoD research funding that was under Title IV[14] provided to: the Army ($12.7 billion or 12%); the Navy ($20.4 billion or 19.4%); the Air Force ($45.7 billion or 43.4%); Defense-wide ($26.3 billion or 25%); and operational test and evaluation ($0.2 billion or 0.2%).[15] The other 3% funded programs in Title VI[16] under the Chemical Agents and Munitions Destruction Program, the Defense Health Program, and the Inspector General. In some instances, RDT&E funding was provided for the National Defense Sealift Fund and OCO.

Even though RDT&E funds are appropriated by organization, the DoD characterizes the RDT&E funds into eight categories. The first three categories – basic research, applied research, and advanced technology development – are viewed as investments in future technology for the development of advanced systems. The next three categories – advanced component development and prototypes, system development and demonstration, and operational systems development – focus on implementing existing technology to support current or near-term needs. Management of RDT&E supports work for research allocated in other budget categories. The category software and digital technology pilot programs is relatively new and was added in the DoD's FY 2021 budget request (Sargent, 2020, p. 5). Figure 9 details the share of funding by character of work.

The DoD is a significant source of funding, providing approximately 40% of total funding for certain university programs such as aerospace, aeronautical, astronautical, electrical, electronic, and communications engineering; around 24% for industrial and manufacturing; 28% for mechanical engineering; 24% for metallurgical and materials sciences; and 30% for computer and information sciences. In fact, the DoD spends almost half of its basic research funding at universities (Sargent, 2020, p. 5).

The level of funding for DoD RDT&E has fluctuated over the past two decades. Between FY 2000 and FY 2007, total funding rose by 73% in constant dollars. Funding remained flat between FY 2007 and FY 2010. It fell by 27% between FY 2010 and FY 2015 and rose by 51% between FY 2015 and FY 2020.

In debating the appropriate funding level for DoD RDT&E, Congress turned to the 1998 Defense Science Board Task Force on the Defense Science and Technology Base for the 21st Century proposal to use industry benchmarks. The industry benchmark is RDT&E share of product sales. Since the DoD does not have sales, it substituted total DoD funding level for sales. The standard level is

---

[14] Title IV funding funds research, development, test, and evaluation for the Army, Navy, Air Force, Space Force, Defense-wide, and Operational Test and Evaluation.

[15] Space Force received no funding in FY 2020.

[16] Title VI funds other defense programs such as chemical agents and munitions destruction; defense health programs; and the Inspector General.

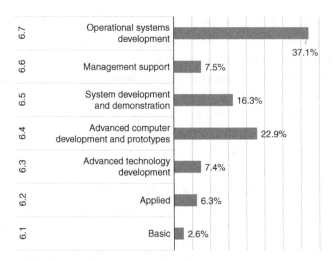

**Figure 9** RDT&E funding by character of work and percentage of funding
**Notes:** The DoD characterizes the RDT&E funding by the character of work to be performed. Each characterization has a budget activity code, 6.1–6.7, and a descriptor. Basic research is study directed toward greater knowledge of the fundamental aspects of issues without specific applications to processes. It is farsighted research that provides the basis for technological progress. Applied research is directed to meet a specific need. It may be oriented to the design and development of prototypes. Advanced technology development includes development of components to integrate subsystems for filed and simulated experiments.
**Source:** Congressional Research Service (2020), data from the DoD FY 2020 RDT&E programs

about 14%. The DoD RDT&E levels fluctuated from a low of 11% to a high of 14.7% between FY 1996 and FY 2020. Figure 10 depicts RDT&E funding as a percentage of DoD funding.

An issue with using this benchmark is that during times of conflict or when the DoD budget increases substantially due to factors such as increase in cost of operations, replacements, and forces, and even though the percentage allocated to RDT&E is stable, the absolute value of funds available for RDT&E will fluctuate. The fluctuations will be mostly unrelated to research needs and demands of the DoD.

Another critical issue is the balance between funding for research focused on incremental or evolutionary improvements and funding for research focused on high-risk, high-reward exploratory research that might lead to groundbreaking technological innovations. The 1998 Defense Science

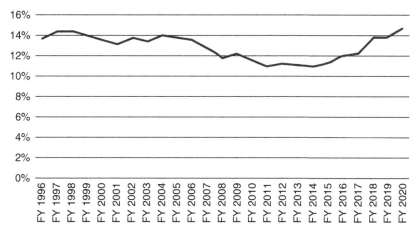

**Figure 10** DoD RDT&E funding as a share of DoD total obligational authority
**Sources:** Sargent (2020, p. 11); Office of the Under Secretary of Defense (2020a)

Board Task Force on the Defense Science and Technology Base for the 21st Century recommended industry's practice of allocating a third of total research funding to exploratory research and two-thirds to evolutionary research. In addition, the National Academies recommended at least 8% of research budgets should be dedicated to evolutionary research. The Defense Advanced Projects Research Agency (DARPA) is the lead DoD agency for exploratory research. Following the Soviet launch of Sputnik, DARPA was established in 1958. However, DARPA funding as a percentage of RDT&E funding has fluctuated, falling from a high of 6.4% in FY 1996 to 3.3% in FY 2020. Clearly, the DoD evolutionary research budget falls far short of recommended levels.

## 4.2 Procurement

For defense-specialized purchases, the government is the sole customer and determines the rules for the market. The more important rules and market characteristics are discussed in this section.

### 4.2.1 Federal Acquisition Regulation

The DoD, like all agencies of the federal government, is guided by the Federal Acquisition Regulation (FAR) in acquiring goods and services and, in some sense, industrial policy is influenced by the FAR. The FAR is jointly published by the General Services Administration (GSA), DoD, and NASA (National Aeronautics and Space Administration) (Federal Acquisition Regulation,

2020a). In addition, some sections of the FAR are supplemented by PGI (Procedures, Guidance, and Information). The FAR is also supplemented by the Defense Federal Acquisition Regulation Supplement (DFARS) as well as the Army (AFAR), Navy (NFAR), and Air Force (AFFAR; Federal Acquisition Regulation, 2020a) The current FAR itself is 1,988 pages, not including the supplements already noted, which include all military services. The FAR system is intended to comprehensively prescribe standard, permissible actions in federal purchase of goods and services – including circumstances in which deviations are authorized.

One effect resulting from the length and complexity of the FAR is the difficulty in dealing with commercial firms in the general economy. A federal forum on managing the defense supplier base observed, "the challenge of operating in accordance with complex federal acquisition regulations discourage small and innovative businesses from partnering with the government," particularly in sectors such as biotechnology (US Government Accountability Office, 2006, p. 7).

Another effect is encouraging defense acquisition through other means to avoid the complexity of the FAR. These means include the Air Force Rapid Capabilities Office, DoD's Strategic Capabilities Office (Franck, Hildebrandt, and Udis, 2016), and using other transactional authorities (OTA; Magnuson, 2018).

The OTA arrangements are authorized in existing legislation for some contracts, and whoever "comes forth to compete for this money can ignore the Federal Acquisition Regulation, the dreaded FAR, and do an end run around its notorious red tape" (Magnuson, 2018). It is fair to say that working around the FAR system, as opposed to reforming the FAR, is likely to be a standard practice for the indefinite future.

The FAR seems to be past a tipping point. It is large, complex, and confusing to potential market entrants. Even though no one encountered in our inquiries extols the FAR's usefulness, it continues to grow: from 1,741 pages in 2018 (US General Services Administration, 2019) to 1,988 pages in 2020 (Federal Acquisition Regulation, 2020a). Those with power to reform the FAR tend to be political appointees who will not be around long enough to accomplish anything meaningful along those lines.

One problem resulting from FAR complexity is poor awareness of federal cybersecurity standards pertaining to contractors. A survey of small and medium-sized defense contractors conducted by the National Defense Industrial Association found that less than 60% of respondents said that they read the Defense FAR Supplement that established security standards for contractor information systems. Nearly half of those who read the FAR said that they found it hard to understand, and approximately 45% did not read the guidelines set in the National Institute for Standards and Technology for protecting controlled unclassified information (Johnson, 2019).

### 4.2.2 Barriers to Entry

> [T]he top tier of the defense industry (is) a nearly impenetrable cadre that is shrinking. (Bruno, 2020, p. 12)

Standard microeconomics holds that a key characteristic of any market is the presence (or not) of significant barriers to entry. A long-standing metric for entry barriers is the cost an aspirant firm must pay to enter a particular market. Basically, entry costs are extra production costs borne by market entrants and not incumbents (Baumol, Panzar, and Willig, 1988, pp. 4–5). Thus, for example, acquiring physical or human capital as a prerequisite to entering a new market results in extra production costs for the entrant but is a cost already borne by the incumbents. As such, this is a cost that affects a decision to enter but not a decision to remain, and is therefore a barrier to entry (Baumol, Panzar, and Willig, 1988, p. 281).

That barrier can be significantly higher in entering the defense market. As Baumol, Panzar, and Willig (1988, p. 289) put it, "in the most regulated industries there is a substantial entry barrier that takes the form of . . . costs and delays to obtain the regulatory agency's permission." Since the defense marketplace is highly regulated, and the sovereign monopsonist is the only customer, the US government is the regulator, and grants permission to enter. Hence, barriers to entry are especially important considerations for the US defense marketplace. But, as one would expect, there are aspects peculiar to this market.

The US DoD sources most of its spending domestically, due to the US defense industry's high competency and the Buy American Act – which sets procurement preference for domestic products with a substantially negative evaluation factor applied to most foreign products – for various reasons, a small share of DoD purchases go to foreign firms (US Government Accountability Office, 2018).

Even though the United States is the leading arms-exporting nation, it is also a major arms importer, ranked 17th in 2019 by SIPRI TIV metrics.[17] It is, however, difficult for foreign defense firms to enter the US market.

Airbus Group's[18] attempt to become a major supplier to the DoD serves as an illustrative example. Airbus Group was (and is) a diversified and profitable

---

[17] SIPRI's primary unit of measurement is TIV, in lieu of direct financial value. See www.sipri.org /databases/milex (accessed: September 8, 2021) for further explanation.

[18] Incorporated as EADS (the European Aeronautic Defence and Space Company) prior to 2014.

enterprise, with a robust portfolio of defense business, and a successful line to commercial air transports. In the first decade of this century, it had substantial resources in multiple dimensions to effect an entry into the US defense market.[19]

Airbus Group entered the twenty-first century with a mixed assessment of future profitability. While the Airbus division was a leading supplier of commercial airliners with European governments' sharing development risks, it was under increasing pressure. The airline market was also cyclical and not consistently profitable.

Airbus set out to increase its defense business by targeting the US market (Defense Industrial Daily, 2005). There were significant barriers to overcome. First were well-established US incumbents with market knowledge, military technology, and political connections. Second were strong "Buy American" statutes. Finally, US–French relations were not cordial at the time. There was, however, room for more firms in the market following the US consolidations in the 1990s. For example, Boeing was the only domestic source for a replacement Air Force aerial tanker (KC-X) – Airbus Group being the most credible alternative.

The Airbus approach was to find a US partner, Northrop–Grumman (NG). The company was, and still is, a major aerospace firm well established in the US market, with associated market knowledge and customer connections within the US government (Franck, Lewis, and Udis, 2008, pp. 106–114, esp. p. 109).

However, this well-conceived and well-supported strategy did not quite succeed. The NG–Airbus Group team won the first KC-X source selection in 2008, but Boeing successfully protested that result, and won the repeated competition in 2011 (Franck and Udis, 2017). Currently, Airbus Group has only limited sales to the DoD.

### 4.2.2.1 BAE: A Conspicuous Exception

The only non-US firm currently among the DoD's largest suppliers is BAE, ranked 12th in 2019 (Aeroweb, 2020a). BAE Systems, a British firm, views the United States as one of its primary markets, and the most promising (BAE Systems, 2020). It is unique among major non-US defense firms. First, BAE participation in the US market has been facilitated by the long-standing special relationship between the UK and the United States. This has included close cooperation in defense acquisition programs, from the atomic bomb to the F-35. Among other things, this traditional cooperation helped BAE establish trust with the DoD. The addition of the UK to the US National Technical Industrial Base (NTIB; Peters, 2021, p. 1) will likely enhance this relationship.

---

[19] In 2002, Airbus Group was ranked 7th in revenue among defense firms, due mostly to its market position in Europe (Aeroweb, 2020a).

Second, BAE's strategy includes acquisitions that strengthen its position in the US market. Examples include Tracor (1999) as part of BAE's merger with Marconi Electronic Systems, (WikiMili, 2020), and Sanders (Wikipedia, 2020). These are two US suppliers of highly classified military equipment. Recently, BAE has acquired business units such as Collins Aerospace Military GPS and Raytheon's Airborne Tactical Radios. These were divestments mandated for approval of the Raytheon-United Technologies (UTC) merger completed in 2020 (BAE Systems, 2019).

Third, BAE has a special security agreement (SSA) with the US government; there's a "firewall" that prevents exchange of highly sensitive information between executives of the US affiliate, all US citizens, and the parent corporation in the UK (summary at BAE Systems, 2020).

Finally, BAE has established a dual-citizenship corporate identity: US citizens have long held a significant portion of its shares (Wayne, 2006); and US citizens occupy four of the ten positions on BAE's Board of Directors. More than a third of BAE's employees are in the United States, which is the largest source (43%) of BAE's revenues (BAE Systems, 2019, pp. 3, 21, 88).

### 4.2.2.2 Cybersecurity: An Example of Barriers to Entering the Supply Chain

Barriers to entry are not limited to the primes. They also apply to the rest of the supply chain. A current concern is cybersecurity. The problem is real and defense industrial cybersecurity could be improved (Johnson, 2019; Office of the Director of National Intelligence, 2020). To deal more effectively with the problem, the DoD proposes a new cybersecurity standard, which is more strict than the current standard in NIST Publication 800-171 (Ross *et al.*, 2020), which has been the DoD standard (Dwyer, 2019).

The supplement is Cybersecurity Maturity Model Certification (CMMC). Its major feature is prescribed levels of cybersecurity intended to fit the level of information handled by various levels and firms in the supply chain (Acquisition and Sustainment, 2020, pp. 3–4). Bidders for DoD contracts will be eligible only if they meet the appropriate CMMC level for themselves and their supply chain (Dwyer, 2019).

Since all incumbents and entrants will be held to the same standard, and have the same costs of compliance, this seems not to be a barrier to entry. However, the DoD has indicated that costs of CMMC compliance will likely be allowable for its suppliers. This probably means that firms with DoD contracts will be reimbursed for their CMMC-related costs. But aspiring entrants have no visible prospects of reimbursement. If not, then they will be kept out of the market until they assume those costs (Dwyer, 2019). CMMC then would be yet another barrier to entry to the defense market – especially for smaller businesses.

The DoD may find ways to ameliorate this unintended consequence, but it is worth noting that specialized defense needs, including security, can result in more barriers to entry.

### 4.2.3 Defense Production Act

The Defense Production Act (DPA) of 1950 is intended to ensure adequate means of responding to emergencies, including wars and natural disasters. The original version contained seven sections or titles, which authorized command economy measures in such emergencies. However, four of those sections lapsed early on (Cecire and Peters, 2020a).

(1) Title I primarily addresses declaration of priority for defense programs, and allocation of resources to execute those programs (Cecire and Peters, 2020a, pp. 5–6).
(2) Title III authorizes financial incentives to increase supply of essential materials for national defense (Cecire and Peters, 2020a, p. 9–14).
(3) Among other things, Title VII mandates Industrial Base Assessments and a Committee on Foreign Investment in the United States (CFIUS; Cecire and Peters, 2020a, p. 14–18).

Recently, the DPA has been invoked to effect responses to the COVID-19 pandemic. One example is "priority rated orders" with drug firms for the large-scale manufacture of supplies for testing, and to ensure timely distribution of those supplies to nursing homes (Cecire and Peters, 2020b; US Department of Health and Human Services, 2020).

Defense Industrial Reports are transmitted to the President and Congress on an annual basis. The latest published (as of this writing) is the US Department of Defense (2018b) *Annual Industrial Capabilities Report to Congress*.

### 4.2.4 Committee on Foreign Investment in the United States

A number of countries are concerned about the national security implications of foreign investment, and have systems in place to monitor, and possibly forbid, foreign investment with significant national security risks (Masters and McBride, 2018). In 1975, the United States formed CFIUS. The committee implements provisions of the Defense Production Act of 1950 and is charged with vetting foreign investments with potential national security implications (US Department of the Treasury, 2020).

The CFIUS mission has become increasingly demanding and complicated, associated with government concerns about the overall effectiveness of the system (Masters and McBride, 2018, p. 2). A tightening of the CFIUS regulatory regime occurred in 1988, with the Exon–Florio Provision, which resulted in a substantially larger role for the committee (Jackson, 2020, pp. 7–8),

In 2007, the Foreign Investment and National Security Act of 2007 (FINSA) provided additional legislative guidance to the CFIUS. Among other things, FINSA adds members to the committee and mandates increased senior-level participation and accountability (US Department of the Treasury, 2008). In 2018, the United States enacted the Foreign Investment Risk Review Modernization Act (FIRMMA), motivated, at least in part, by fears of the People's Republic of China's "weaponized investment" (Masters and McBride, 2018). Following FIRMMA enactment, CFIUS rejected several investments under FINSA, such as the 2018 proposal involving MoneyGram of Dallas, Texas and Ant FinancialMoney, a Chinese company (Yoon-Hendricks, 2018). More recently, Broad Comm's (incorporated in Singapore) proposed purchase of QualComm was not approved (The White House, 2018a).

### 4.2.5 Profit Policy

> [R]egulations that are detailed, all-encompassing, and arcane ... determine the prices that defense contractors will receive for their products. These regulations are often referred to as ... "profit policy." (Rogerson, 1992, p. 5)

The nature of the defense marketplace necessitates such profit policies. The DoD regularly acquires specialized, high-technology products. These lead to a monopsonist purchasing from a sole-source supplier. Being sovereign, the government can make the rules and does. Since there is no market price available, the government negotiates a suitable price for the product in accordance with a profit policy (Rogerson, 1992).

However, suppliers must (of course) pay all of the costs that they incur, but government policy does not allow some of them. Hence, "profit" defined by the government is not the same as the profit experienced by the suppliers – that is, net income. According to the FAR (Federal Acquisition Regulation, 2020b, section 15), "profit" is the result of a "fee negotiation" and is "total remuneration ... over and above *allowable* costs" (emphasis added).

However, the sovereign monopsonist recognizes responsibility for a healthy industrial base – by, among other things, offering the prospect of financial rewards that "stimulate efficient contract performance," "attract ... qualified ... business concerns," and "maintain a viable industrial base" (Federal Acquisition Regulation, 2020b, section 15).

### 4.2.5.1 Profit Policy Issues

There is good reason to conclude that the DoD's profit policy in practice maintains a viable industrial base. A study by the Institute for Defense Analyses (IDA; Arnold *et al.*, 2008) offered persuasive evidence of the DoD's profit policy's sustainability – "profits of the major defense contractors are above the levels required to keep them in the defense industrial base" (p. S-4) – and financial viability – "the defense industrial base has performed very well for most of the past 20 years" (p. 48).

It is less certain that the DoD's policy supports entry of new firms to the DIB, especially tech firms. Loren Thompson[20] offered a striking list of reasons "why Silicon Valley won't partner with the Pentagon." Heading that list was profit – "the margins are lousy" (Thompson, 2015). Nonetheless, big tech firms seem to be eager to compete on large information technology (IT) defense programs like JEDI (Joint Enterprise Defense Infrastructure) and ABMS (Advanced Battle Management System).[21]

Moreover, profit policy restrictions can be avoided, as a chapter in TransDigm's corporate history illustrates.

### 4.2.5.2 TransDigm's Profit Margins: A Case in Point

TransDigm Group, Inc. is primarily a supplier of commercial and military aerospace components. It is 32nd in the 2020 *DefenseNews* Top 100 and reports 37% of its revenue from defense business after its acquisition of Esterline Technologies in 2019 (PR Newswire, 2019). Its corporate strategy is aimed, in good part, toward dominating the market for selected types of horseshoe nails,[22] figuratively speaking. TransDigm has sought, and often successfully, to become a sole-source supplier or monopolist for parts. It reports a "unique business model" in which "about 80% of our sales come from products for which we believe we are the sole source provider" (e.g., TransDigm Incorporated, 2017, p. 3). Acquiring Esterline was intended to bolster "TransDigm's platform of proprietary and sole source content for the aerospace and defense industries" (PR Newswire, 2019).

---

[20] Dr. Thompson, Lexington Institute, is an effective advocate for the institute's industrial sponsors. This makes him a useful source here.

[21] We discuss this in more detail while assessing the current state of competition in the defense marketplace.

[22] Small, frequently overlooked things that can be very important, from a poem attributed to Benjamin Franklin (www.citadel.edu/root/images/commandant/assistant-commandant-leadership/for-the-want-of-a-nail.pdf [accessed: September 8, 2021]). The point here is that a well-informed quartermaster of the army in question would have been willing to pay a high price to get a replacement horseshoe nail.

Accordingly, TransDigm has made corporate acquisitions that establish a monopoly position in selected parts and components. Following these acquisitions, profit margins for these items have increased dramatically and resulted in excess profits for 46 of the 47 parts in the investigation's sample (US Department of Defense Office of the Inspector General, 2019). It is especially interesting that the Inspector General found that the contracting officers involved had followed established procedures and exercised due diligence in negotiations (US Department of Defense Office of the Inspector General, 2019).

This was apparently accomplished by:

(1) staying below contract values requiring heightened scrutiny; and
(2) opaque market arrangements in which the source of the TransDigm parts was not evident: "TransDigm was the only manufacturer at the time for a number of parts supplied through contracts competitively awarded; this afforded TransDigm an opportunity to set the market price for those parts because the other competitors planned to buy the parts from TransDigm before selling them to the DLA" (US Department of Defense Office of the Inspector General, 2019).

Among the Inspector General recommendations was the need to "consider all available corrective actions with TransDigm" (US Department of Defense Office of the Inspector General, 2019). TransDigm voluntarily returned $16.1 million, without admission of wrongdoing (Dayen, 2019). This seems to be yet another example of regulated companies being motivated to seek ways to avoid the regulators.

## 4.3 The Defense Export Control Regime

The United States is a major exporter of defense goods and services. Military sales, however, can have consequences beyond the transaction itself. Accordingly, the US government considers a variety of national security and other policy goals in controlling military exports (Directorate of Defense Trade Controls, 2020a). The legislative foundations for the export control regime include the Arms Export Control Act (AECA) of 1976 and the Export Administration Act (EAA) of 1979. While three federal departments (State, Commerce, and Treasury) issue export licenses, Defense, Homeland Security, and the Intelligence Community are also involved in the controls system. The State Department's ITAR (International Traffic in Arms Regulations) and the Department of Commerce's Export Administration Regulations (EAR) contain the rules for administering the export control regime.

The ITAR system applies, basically, to US persons who wish to sell munitions or other goods and services with national security implications to non-US persons. Any potential exporters of military goods must register with the Directorate of Defense Trade Controls (Directorate of Defense Trade Controls, 2020b) and obtain appropriate export authorizations, which include restrictions on retransfer and reexports. Retransfer authorizations are generally as time consuming as the original authorization.

The system includes Congressional oversight. The Executive Branch must provide advance notice to Congress regarding proposed arms sales. Congress may then pass legislation to block or modify the sale at any time prior to delivery of the items in question (Kerr, 2020, summary) Congress can block sales by legislation and there is reason to believe that Congress's role is greater in practice.

US export controls are frequently perceived as irksome and counterproductive, especially by customers.

- A French view: "We are at the mercy of the Americans. Is that satisfactory? No. But we don't have any choice" (Florence Parly, French minister of defense, quoted in Reuters, 2018a).[23]
- A British conclusion: "I would encourage UK industry to design around the U.S. International Trafficking in Arms Regulations (ITAR) and produce ITAR-free items" (James Arbuthnot, Chair of the UK House of Parliament Select Defense Committee, quoted in Moore *et al.*, 2011).

However, export controls have benefits such as avoiding negative outcomes, and are difficult to enumerate, much less quantify – apart from anecdotal information. The United States prevented Venezuela's export of F-16 fighter aircraft to Iran, a US adversary (CBS News, 2006). It also prevented sales of air transports to Venezuela in that same year (Associated Press, 2006).

Lack of enforceable controls can be costly. According to a number of reports (e.g., Page, 2010), the Chinese purchased Russian tactical fighters in the 1990s and have exploited those sales in ways counter to Russian interests. For example, China ordered 24 Su-27s from Russia in 1992. In 1996, the two countries reached an agreement for licensed production of 200 Su-27s (called the J-11). In 2004, the Chinese cancelled the contract after completing half of the license agreement. Fairly soon thereafter, China introduced the J-11B with 90% domestic content, according to official statements. Those Chinese tactical fighters then actively competed against Russian exports. As one Russian official

---

[23] This particular statement (2018) referred to MQ-9 Reaper unmanned air vehicles carrying weapons. Subsequently, the Trump Administration announced substantially fewer restrictions on exports of armed Reapers (and similar vehicles).

put it, "we didn't pay enough attention to our intellectual property" (Page, 2010).

For the private-sector participants, the direct costs of export controls include processing authorization requests. Boeing, for example, had about 100 full-time employees dealing with ITAR matters in the *commercial* Boeing 787 program (Gates, 2006).

Some costs associated with the export control system are also difficult to quantify. They include worsened relations with long-standing military allies like the UK and France, as noted in the previous quotes.

Perhaps the most serious costs are distortions in behavior of both customers and producers. US allies report that they are seriously considering reducing military relations, equipment purchases, and joint production with the United States in order to avoid the ITAR regime (Reuters, 2018a). The effects go beyond military exports. For example, Boeing resorted to some rather exotic and expensive measures to lessen its 787 airliner's exposure to ITAR (Gates, 2006).

### 4.3.1 Reform of the Export Control Regime

> At some point people need to lift their eyes . . . and look around at how the global market has changed. (Loren Thompson, quoted in Gates, 2006)

Some US government agencies, such as the GAO, have expressed dissatisfaction with the export control regime (US Government Accountability Office, 2007). In August 2009, during the first term of the Obama Administration, the President directed a comprehensive review of export controls. The review concluded that the current system was seriously broken. The overarching recommendation was to refocus the effort to better protect really critical technologies – the "crown jewels" (The White House, 2010). The recommendations, with President Obama's approval, also focused on moving to a single control list, a single primary enforcement agency, a single licensing agency, and a single IT system. Implementation measures included two executive orders (The White House, 2010, 2013). However, full implementation of these reforms remains unfinished business. For example, "(t)he Administration made no specific proposals concerning the single licensing agency . . . (but) implemented some elements of a future single system" (Fergusson and Kerr, 2020, summary).

The Trump Administration also undertook export reform initiatives, but with different policy priorities. A new conventional arms transfer (CAT) policy was introduced (The White House, 2018b) and the administration undertook a number of initiatives to encourage export of US arms, such as the Export Control Reform Act of 2018 (US Congress, 2018). Specific measures include approving exports not permitted in the Obama Administration, such as F-16s to

Taiwan, (McBride, 2019) and recent liberalization of exports of armed unmanned air vehicles (UAVs), enabled by a revised interpretation of the missile export control regime announced in July 2020 (WorldECR, 2020). Potential customers of US arms have seen efforts toward faster approvals (Aviation Week, 2020, p. 8), tailored payment schedules (Mehta, 2020a), and reduced administrative fees (Mehta, 2020b).

The practical effects included a significant increase in approved requests for foreign military sales for 2018 and beyond (Mehta, 2018b) and strengthened the US role in the international arms trade (SIPRI, 2019). However, it is too soon to predict the long-term effects of these initiatives. Also, other factors are involved, such as increased tension in the Middle East and Indo-Pacific regions. Finally, given the shifts in export control policy with changes in US administrations, it is unclear what will happen with the new administration.

## 5 Defense Industrial Consolidation Post-Cold War

In 1993, Secretary of Defense Aspin and Deputy Secretary Perry concluded that some industrial consolidation was necessary and announced this to executives from major defense companies at a Pentagon dinner.[24] The main message was that the major defense players needed to consolidate to survive and the DoD would facilitate the process by offering financial incentives and advocating consolidations in the event of antitrust challenges. The audience was receptive and as Norman Augustine put it later: "You weren't going to survive unless you were willing to combine. So, there was not much of a choice" (Aitoro, 2016).

The administration delivered and provided strong advocacy for the Boeing–McDonnell Douglas merger. It also allowed reorganization expenses as part of reimbursable costs. All this amounted to significant support, both direct and indirect, for consolidation (Gartzke, 2010, pp. 114, 116).

Many mergers and acquisitions followed. One source (Tirpak, 1998) estimated that 51 defense companies were combined into five. Reportedly, the financial value of the major 1990s consolidations totaled $55 billion (Wayne, 1998b). The marquee mergers were Northrop with Grumman (in April 1994), Lockheed with Martin Marietta (in August 1994), and Boeing with McDonnell Douglas (in December 1996).

The era of very large mergers came to a rather abrupt end in 1998. With the proposed merger of Lockheed–Martin and Northrop–Grumman, and the advent of new leadership at the Departments of Justice and Defense, a consensus emerged that a merger between Lockheed–Martin and Northrop–Grumman

---

[24] The dinner became known as the "Last Supper."

went too far. Wayne (1998b), and Ricks and Cole (1998) provide excellent contemporaneous reporting of these events.

We view the "Last Supper" as ratifying, encouraging, and accelerating a long-term trend toward consolidation in defense industries. "Eye charts" showing defense corporations merging into ever smaller numbers have regularly depicted this phenomenon (e.g., Bialos, Fisher, and Koehl, 2009, p. 639; Hoff, 2007, pp. 51–55).

## 5.1 Industrial Response to the Last Supper Mandate

As could be expected, defense industry responses to the DoD's Last Supper (1993) invitation to merge varied with position in the market, and other things. Some chose to get bigger through mergers and acquisitions; some to get smaller; and others to diversify into commercial markets.[25]

The predominant response for defense industrial firms was to get larger for economies of scale, among other things. This resulted in some large mergers and acquisitions, as noted earlier. More recently, L3 Communications, ranked 8th in 2017, and Harris, at 20th, merged to form L3Harris in 2019; Raytheon, ranked 4th in 2019, and UTC, at 17th, merged as Raytheon Technologies in 2020.

Perhaps the most interesting response came from General Dynamics (GD). In 1991, the firm was a major US defense contractor (2nd in DoD sales, with 82% of its revenue from defense work). It had a broad defense portfolio: submarines, tanks, fighter aircraft, satellite launch vehicles (SLVs), tactical missiles, and communications. However, it was headed for serious financial trouble, with reduced orders at the end of the Cold War (Murphy and Dial, 1993, pp. 3–7).

During the period 1991–1994, GD, as part of a survival strategy, sold off major assets, contracting to the firm's core business lines. GD sold its military aircraft business (F-16s) to Lockheed in 1993; space systems to Martin Marietta in 1993; missiles to Hughes Aircraft in 1992; and communications to Carlyle Group in 1992 (FundingUniverse, 2020; Murphy and Dial, 1993, p. 5).

By the end of the divestment period, GD's defense business portfolio was reduced to submarines and tanks (FundingUniverse, 2020). There was a later report that GD seriously considered selling off all of its assets, cashing out the company.[26] However, after 1994, GD shifted from focused contraction into expansion by acquisitions, which has persisted, as Table 2 illustrates.[27] This

---

[25] Our inquiries did not reveal any major defense industrial concern that chose to follow business as usual.

[26] We consider this credible, but not verified.

[27] Two things worth noting: (1) GDs period of divestment was during the tenure of William Anders as a major GD executive (vice chair, chair and CEO, and chair, from 1990 to 1994; Murphy and

**Table 2** Snapshot views of GD's defense divisions

| 1990 | 1994 | 2020 |
|---|---|---|
| Military aircraft (primarily F-16s) | To Lockheed | |
| Nuclear submarines | Core business retained | Marine systems (submarines, surface combatants, and support ships) |
| Tanks | Core business retained | Combat systems (family of combat vehicles and ordnance products) |
| Space systems | To Martin Marietta | |
| Missiles | To Hughes Aircraft | |
| Electronics (communications gear) | To Carlyle Group | Mission systems (C4ISR integration) |
| | | IT (training systems, commercial services)[a] |

**Note:** [a] A new GD division.
**Sources:** General Dynamics (2020); Murphy and Dial (1993, p. 5)

started with Bath Iron Works in 1995 (FundingUniverse, 2020). GD remains a major defense firm (6th; DefenseNews, 2019), with 66% of its revenues coming from defense sales.

Some companies decided to diversify, Rockwell International, a major defense firm during the Cold War, committed to diversifying its business prior to 1989: "In a changing economic climate for military aerospace manufacturers, Rockwell ... headed toward genuine diversification, away from government-funded contracts" (Reference for Business, 2020).

But Rockwell eventually exited the defense market. Boeing acquired a significant amount of Rockwell International's defense business in 1996 (Cole and Lipin, 1996). Rockwell Collins, spun off in 2001, was acquired by UTC in 2018.[28] As an independent firm, most of the former Rockwell International is Rockwell Automation, a mainly commercial enterprise.

---

Dial, 1993); and (2) the shift to growth-by-acquisition occurred when defense, research and development, and procurement expenditures stopped decreasing in the mid-1990s.

[28] UTC merged with Raytheon in 2020. The story of mergers, acquisitions, and spinoffs in the US defense industry is rather complicated.

## 5.2 Effects of Consolidation: The Ground Based Strategic Deterrent Program

The previous discussion indicates DIB consolidation post-1993 proceeded well and with satisfactory results. However, an overall assessment is more complex. The ground based strategic deterrent (GBSD) offers a different perspective (Global Security, 2020a).

GBSD is a new intercontinental ballistic missile (ICBM) program intended to replace the Minuteman, which has been operational since 1962. However, the number of firms with capabilities to support ICBM production and sustainment has reduced considerably over those decades. The ongoing GBSD program reveals the significance of fewer suppliers, particularly in large solid rocket motors (SRMs).

The discussion begins with some background to provide context: a brief history of the Minuteman ICBM with focus on potential suppliers for large SRMs. It then discusses the GBSD, its rationale, and progress. Next, it covers the competition, with one of two potential suppliers (e.g., Boeing) electing not to bid. Finally, it assesses the situation as of this writing.

### 5.2.1 Minuteman ICBM

The Minuteman ICBM was first deployed in 1962 (Minuteman Missile, 2011). By the mid-1970s, 1,000 missiles were deployed in hardened silos: Minuteman IIs (MMIIs; 450), and MMIIIs (550; Global Security, 2020b). With the end of the Cold War, breakup of the Soviet Union, and associated nuclear arms control agreements, the number of deployed missiles decreased to 400 MMIIIs (Harrison and Linck, 2017, esp. figure 4, p. 4).

The MMIII has been deployed since 1970, with associated aging and obsolescence issues (Global Security, 2020b). However, upgrade and life-extension programs have dealt with many of them. The programs included the Minuteman integrated life-extension program (RIVET Mile), begun in 1985 (Flfrick, 2005). Other life-extension programs began in the late 1990s.

Of particular note was the propulsion replacement program (PRP). To extend reliable service life, PRP replaced the solid rocket fuel to include remanufacture of the third stage. Work began in 1998, with NG as the lead contractor, and was complete in 2013 (Woolf, 2019, p. 14). Rocket motors for all three stages were repoured or replaced, with Alliant Techsystems (ATK) providing the rocket motors (Aeroweb, 2020b; Woolf, 2019, p. 14).

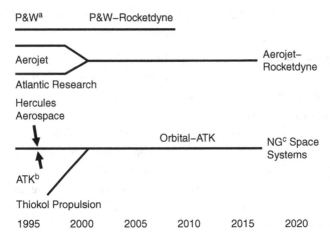

**Figure 11** Consolidation in US SRM firms over the past quarter century
**Notes:** (a) Pratt & Whitney; (b) Alliant Techsystems; (c) Northrop Grumman
**Source:** Adapted from US Government Accountability Office (2017, p. 9)

### 5.2.2 Defense Industrial Base: SRM Sector

During the Cold War, there was sufficient demand for SRMs to keep a number of suppliers in business. Demand collapsed in the 1990s and declined still more with the termination of NASA's space shuttle program (Erwin, 2018a). Accordingly, the number of US firms capable of producing SRMs declined to two, as shown in Figure 11. The DoD's Annual Industrial Capabilities Report for FY 2017 flagged this sector as being of highest risk (US Department of Defense, 2018b, esp. pp. 41, 105).[29]

Orbital Sciences, which incorporated in 1982, is of particular interest. Notable among its acquisitions was ATK's aerospace and defense divisions in 2015 (Crunchbase, 2020). ATK was 37th in the *DefenseNews* Top 100 in 2014. Orbital–ATK was, in turn, acquired by NG for $9.2 billion, including assumption of $1.4 billion in debt, and was approved on June 5, 2018 (Erwin, 2018a). Both corporations had announced their intentions on July 18, 2017 Northrop–Grumman and Orbital–ATK, 2017).[30]

However, the Orbital–ATK acquisition came with conditions, primarily nondiscrimination for Orbital's SRM business (summarized in a Federal Trade Commission [FTC] press release; Federal Trade Commission, 2018a). The enlarged NG Corporation was specifically enjoined to deal with third-party firms like Boeing exactly the same as it would for business within the firm

---

[29] However, the FY 2018 report discussed efforts to mitigate this situation (US Department of Defense, 2019, esp. pp. 82, 85).

[30] This occurred at roughly the same time that NG learned it was still in the running for GBSD.

(nondiscrimination) with strict protection for customers' proprietary information (firewalls, and FTC decision and order; Federal Trade Commission, 2018b, esp. paragraphs I A and J; II A; III A, B, and D).

In particular, the directed nondiscrimination provisions included the following:

- SRMs and related services should be made available to all potential customers, including NG's competitors;
- firewalls should be established to prevent the transfer of proprietary information of those competitors; and
- the DoD directed the appointment of a compliance officer to oversee NG compliance with the FTC decision and order (Federal Trade Commission, 2018a).

As one observer (Erwin, 2018a) put it: "Ensuring competition in the solid rocket motors industry is a key issue for the Defense Department … The FTC decision requires Northrop Grumman to separate its solid rocket motors business with a firewall so it can continue to support Boeing. It will be up to the Defense Department to ensure compliance with the firewall mandate."

### 5.2.3 GBSD Development and Source Selection Process

Modernizing the ICBM force, or not, has been a decades-long issue within the DoD, and defense policy circles in general.[31] However, there is now reason to believe that the Minuteman is reaching the end of its operational life and a new ICBM is needed.[32] A particularly troubling issue is the diminishing stock of spare missiles for periodic operational testing, with none expected to be available after 2040 with current test launch rates (Harrison and Linck, 2017). Finally, some studies have concluded that "critical Minuteman III capabilities … cannot be sustained much past the year 2030" (Gunzinger, Rehberg, and Evans, 2018).

With current force deterioration no later than 2030 (Trimble, 2019), the Air Force regards the GBSD as a program of growing urgency. With GBSD initial operational capacity expected in 2027, then at least some Minuteman missiles will deteriorate prior to replacement missiles being ready – that is, GBSD is already "late to need" (Maj. Gen. Michael Fortney, quoted in Trimble, 2019).

---

[31] In the 1980s, for example, programs for two new ICBMs were under way: Peacekeeper and Small ICBM. With the end of the Cold War and subsequent arms control agreements, Peacekeeper was retired (Boese, 2005) and Small ICBM was cancelled (Encyclopedia Astronautica, 2019). This left MMIII as the only remaining ICBM type in service.

[32] Not all informed sources share this opinion, as shown for example in a Center for Strategic and International Studies debate on the subject (CSIS, 2017).

Yet another source of urgency was the perceived need, in a bureaucratic and political sense, for launching the program as soon as possible, especially prior to the 2020 general election (Rick Berger, American Enterprise Institute, quoted in Cohen, 2019).

In 2016, the Air Force announced its intention to replace the Minuteman with GBSD (FAS, 2019). At that point, Boeing, NG, and Lockheed–Martin were in the running for source selection (Carlson, 2017). The planned ICBM effort includes the missile, a reentry vehicle, aeroshell, and silo refurbishment. Other programs will develop and produce a new warhead and modernized command-and-control system (Trimble, 2019).

On August 21, 2017, the Air Force narrowed firms considered to Boeing and NG with contracts for Technical Maturity and Risk Reduction of three years duration awarded to each (Carlson, 2017; Department of Defense, 2017). As noted, NG and Orbital–ATK announced their intention to combine about the same time (July 2017). Acquisition of Orbital–ATK was completed on June 5, 2018.

On July 16, 2019, the Air Force issued a request for proposal (RFP) for the Engineering and Manufacturing Development, of the GBSD (summarized in Bryant, 2019). Shortly thereafter (July 25), Boeing announced its intention to withdraw. The chief reason stated was an unequal contest shaped by NG's acquisition of Orbital–ATK, which gave it the most credible source of large SRMs in the United States (Weisgerber, 2019, as discussed earlier). Accordingly, Boeing claimed a severe disadvantage in preparing a credible offer by the suspense date (Erwin, 2019). As Thompson (2019) put it, "Why should (Boeing) bid on a program (it) can't win?"

In effect, Boeing charged NG with not following the FTC decision and order of December 3, 2018, and mentioned its concern over the matter. The FTC started an investigation (Cordell, 2019), with Boeing promising full cooperation (Clark, 2019). NG acknowledged a demand for information from the FTC (Censer, 2019).

### 5.2.4 The GBSD Situation Post Boeing

At present, the Air Force is continuing the program as planned, with NG chosen as prime contractor (Cohen, 2020). Even optimists (Rehberg, 2019) do not think a sole-source procurement for a program this size is a good situation. While the DoD has expressed confidence in the Air Force's ability to successfully manage the process (Gould, 2019), there are significant obstacles.

Something significant happens when a negotiation ends in a contract. The situation goes from being a competitive market transaction to something like a bilateral monopoly; Williamson (1996, p. 60) calls this a fundamental transformation of the business relationship: "the terms upon which an initial bargain can be struck depend on whether non-collusive bids can be elicited from more than one qualified supplier."

Accordingly, the DoD entered the negotiation with much bargaining leverage already gone. Indeed, a recent survey of Air Force contracting personnel indicated that in sole-source negotiations, they "feel they operate at a negotiating disadvantage" with "power asymmetry between them and the sole-source contractor" (Hartmann *et al.*, 2020).[33] Given the DoD's view of GBSD as an urgent need, it would be difficult for the government to credibly invoke its remaining main negotiating lever of walking away.

Given that sole-source procurement for a large acquisition program is not preferred, some consideration of how that situation arose is worth discussing. It appears that a major root cause is the ongoing consolidation in the US DIB. In general, the DoD "weapons buyers … have the impossible task of running a competitive marketplace when there are, at best, two or three potential suppliers for the most expensive weapons systems." A White House report released last year found 300 cases in which important defense products are produced by just a single company, a fragile supplier, or a foreign supplier (Gregg, 2019).

Following the Cold War, the number of domestic SRMs providers reduced to two. Furthermore, only one of the surviving firms, Orbital–ATK, had large SRM manufacturing capability in place (US Government Accountability Office, 2017). Hence, NG's acquisition of Orbital–ATK rendered prospects for meaningful GBSD competition problematic (Erwin, 2019).

### 5.2.5 Potential Complications Still Ahead

First, and as already noted, the FTC has begun an investigation of NG's compliance with the merger conditions ordered in December 2018 (Weisgerber, 2019). The Worst case for the GBSD program schedule is the FTC concluding that NG engaged in a conspiracy in restraint of trade that the DoD allowed to proceed despite the FTC order for a DoD compliance officer.[34]

Second, Congressional pushback seems guaranteed, due if nothing else to the Chair of the House Armed Services Committee (HASC) being from Washington State. Rep. Adam Smith (D, WA) has already promised special attention to GBSD in its current state, especially the "troubling" process (Erwin, 2019; Gould, 2019).[35] That said, there are some mixed signals. Rep. Anthony Brown, Vice Chair of

---

[33] Readers will undoubtedly note major differences in perspective between the respondents and studies such as Carril and Duggan (2018, pp. 1, 2), cited later.

[34] However, the authors have found no public statements issued in the past year about this matter.

[35] There is a rather long tradition of Washington's Members of Congress being "from Boeing." Examples include Sen. Henry "Scoop" Jackson and Rep. Norman "Norm" Dicks.

HASC, has stated that strategic nuclear forces, especially ICBM, need recapitalization (O'Hanlon *et al.*, 2020).

However, Congress has generally supported GBSD funding, so far (e.g, House Armed Services Committee, 2020, pp. 2688, 2766, 4219, 4423). The House voted by a supermajority against an amendment to reduce that funding, with Chair Smith voting in favor (Defense Daily Staff, 2020).

Finally, the current situation[36] may provide additional support for the alternative of doing another life extension for the MMIII force and accepting less capability. The Chair of HASC states that he is sympathetic to that proposal (Gould, 2019). Along these lines, the current administration announced its intention to review strategic nuclear modernization programs (including GBSD), with a view to reducing expenditures (Reif, 2021).

## 5.3 Consolidation: Current State

The 1998 disapproval of the NG/Lockheed–Martin merger established a precedent that discouraged mergers of the largest companies. This prevailed for about two decades, during which time there was plenty of activity – mostly acquiring smaller companies. But recent experience indicates another era of large-scale consolidations. One industry observer (Bruno, 2020, p. 7) stated "the dam is breaking." According to Harris Chair and CEO, Bill Brown, "There's definitely a need for greater investment, which requires scale" (Mattioli, Cimilluca, and Cameron, 2018). Throughout this complicated period of mergers, acquisitions, spinoffs, and reorganizations, the relative position of the major defense suppliers has been remarkably stable, as shown in Table 3.

**Table 3** Stability of revenue rankings for large US defense firms

| Company | 2019 rank | 2010 rank | 2000 rank |
| --- | --- | --- | --- |
| Lockheed–Martin | 1 | 1 | 1 |
| Boeing | 2 | 3 | 3 |
| NG | 3 | 4 | 4 |
| Raytheon | 4 | 6 | 2 |
| GD | 6 | 5 | 5 |
| UTC | 17 | 10 | 10 |
| L3 Communications[a] | 18 | 9 | 46 |
| General Electric or GE Aviation | 29 | 18 | 5 |

**Note:** [a] Merger with Harris complete in July 2019.
**Source:** DefenseNews (2019)

---

[36] ... which includes significant pressures on defense budgets.

Table 4 shows a representative sample of recent, as of 2019, and noteworthy mergers and acquisitions among the top 100 defense industrial firms. Five of the transactions involved companies that are both listed in the top 100 firms. Other mergers, such as Boeing's acquisition of KLX, have significant transaction values.

The large-scale transactions are not limited to large firms. The merger of TransDigm and Esterline, for example, detailed in Table 4, did not involve any top-tier defense companies. However, both were active in the defense market and the transaction value was certainly significant at $4 billion.

In addition, there were multiple merger and acquisitions involving the same companies. Rockwell Collins, for example, acquired B/E Aerospace in 2017, and then, UTC acquired Rockwell Collins the following year. So, while big five mergers are apparently still off limits, other consolidations are now in play.

An important qualification applies. There is some reason to believe that the Biden Administration could take a more skeptical view of defense industry mergers (Sindreu, 2020).

## 5.4 Acquisitions after 2000: An Illustrative Example

In 1994, Northrop Aircraft acquired Grumman Corporation, and formed Northrop–Grumman. In 2000, NG was ranked 6th in the *DefenseNews* Top 100, with 64% of its revenues coming from defense business. Although NG considers commercial projects integral to its business strategy (Hoyle, 2006), defense revenue percentage increased to 84% in 2019, becoming the third largest defense supplier (DefenseNews, 2019).

After its formation in 1994, NG chose a mix of acquisition and divestment (spinoff). Selected transactions for NG appear in Table 5.

As indicated in Table 5, NG moved relatively quickly to get bigger in 1994. It made major acquisitions in electronics, space systems, and shipbuilding. However, it divested its shipbuilding divisions in 2011, reportedly based on a negative assessment of its position in the shipbuilding market, shipbuilding within the NG corporate structure, and the shipbuilding market in general (Jacobs, 2011). In short, NG's get-bigger strategy was flexible, and could accommodate major changes of direction.

## 5.5 Consolidation: An Assessment

A major architect of the Last Supper[37] initiative, Deputy Secretary of Defense at that time, William Perry,[38] assessed consolidation as a disappointment (Erwin,

---

[37] The "Last Supper" dinner event occurred on July 21, 1993 at the Pentagon (Shelsby, 1995).

[38] Deputy Secretary of Defense, February 1993–February 1994; Secretary of Defense, February 1994–January 1997.

**Table 4** Some recent and noteworthy defense industrial mergers and acquisitions activity

| Firms with top 100 rankings[a] | Type of transaction | Transaction value (billion $) | Announced | Sources |
|---|---|---|---|---|
| Boeing (5) and Millennium Space Systems | Acquisition | Undisclosed | 2018 | Erwin (2018c) |
| Boeing (5) and KLX | Acquisition | 3.2 | 2018 | Boeing (2018) and Kalia (2018) |
| GD (6) and CSRA (39) | Acquisition | 9.6 | 2018 | Mehta (2018a) |
| Harris (19) and L3 Communications (12) | Merger | 15 | 2018 | Mattioli, Cimilluca, and Cameron (2018) |
| NG (5) and Orbital–ATK (31) | Acquisition | 9.2[a] | 2017 | Federal Trade Commission (2018a) |
| Rockwell Collins (40) and B/E Aerospace | Acquisition | 6 | 2017 | Brothers (2017) |
| UTC (12) and Rockwell Collins (40) | Acquisition | 23 | 2017 | Reuters (2018b) |
| TransDigm and Esterline | Acquisition | 4 | 2018 | Esterline Technologies Corporation (2018) |
| SAIC (35) and Engility (79) | Acquisition | 2.5 | 2018 | Mehta (2019) |
| UTC (17) and Raytheon (3) | Merger | 33.6 | 2019 | Thompson (2019) |
| LM (1) and Sikorsky[b] | Acquisition | 9 | 2015 | Thompson (2019) |

**Note:** [a] *DefenseNews* Top 100 ranks indicated at year of announcement. [b] Spinoff from UTC, 2015.

**Table 5** Northrop–Grumman: Selected acquisition and divestment activity through 2019

| Year | Target | Action | Comments | Source |
|------|--------|--------|----------|--------|
| 1996 | Westinghouse Electronic Systems | Acquisition | Radar systems | Mintz (1997) |
| 1997 | Logicon | Acquisition | Defense computers | FundingUniverse (2020) |
| 2001 | Litton Industries | Acquisition | Shipbuilding | Schneider (2001) |
| 2001 | Newport News Shipbuilding | Acquisition | Ships | Merle (2001) |
| 2002 | TRW | Acquisition | Space and laser systems | Wait (2002) |
| 2005 | EADS | Joint proposal | KC-30 aerial tanker proposal | Defense Industrial Daily (2005) |
| 2006 | Boeing | Joint proposal | Spacecraft | Borenstein (2006) |
| 2011 | Huntington Ingalls Industries | Spinoff | NG's shipbuilding facilities | Jacobs (2011) |
| 2017 | Orbital–ATK | Acquisition | Large SRM manufacturing | Federal Trade Commission (2018a) |

2015). "The response we were seeking was a reduction in overhead," Perry said. "What we got was the consolidation of the defense industry, few large companies, and less effective competition" plus continued high overhead costs." Further, consolidation "has the potential to affect innovation, limit the supply base, pose entry barriers ... and ultimately reduce competition resulting in higher prices to be paid by the American taxpayer" (Erwin, 2015).

It is worthwhile digging deeper and considering these asserted outcomes. The industrial base would shrink in the 1990s regardless of policies in place. There were too many firms for post-Cold War defense needs. Barring restructuring, the result would be inadequate return on capital, with suppliers inevitably downsizing or exiting. However, the effects of a prolonged period of adjustment could well: (1) result in a scattering of human capital, and (2) lead to an industrial base ill-suited to post-Cold War needs (Deutch, 2001, esp., pp. 137, 147, 148). Clearly, the relevant policy question was not whether the number of defense firms would decrease, but by how much, how quickly, and to what end state?

A right sized, and structured, DIB would (1) be more efficient particularly with less overhead expenses, (b) sufficiently competitive, and (2) release productive resources to the general economy (Deutch, 2001, p. 138). One important result would be lower acquisition costs relative to the alternatives.

## 5.6 The Last Supper Initiative's Goals

In assessing outcomes, it is useful to consider the consolidation goals. Three people closely associated with the Last Supper, and what followed, provide clear, albeit not fully consistent, statements of those goals.

First is William Perry, who had much to do with the Last Supper meeting. Years later, Prof. Perry stated that the primary goal was to reduce the cost of defense acquisitions by "*compelling* the (defense) industry to become leaner" (emphasis added, Erwin, 2015).[39] Reduced overhead costs were the primary metric for "leaner."

Second is John Deutch,[40] who provided a late-1990s perspective: "the public objective is to assure a defense industrial base ... that meets our security needs" (p. 148). Among other things, this meant financially viable firms delivering high-quality items to the DoD (Deutch, 2001, pp. 138–139).

According to Deutch (2001), achieving an appropriately sized and structured industrial base required active government involvement in:

---

[39] Erwin's words in the article are likely a paraphrase of Perry's statement.
[40] Undersecretary of Defense (Acquisition and Technology), April 1993–May 1994; Deputy Secretary of Defense, March 1994–May 1995.

(1) expediting the process by actively promoting mergers and leading the reorganization of the industrial base: "If the government does not take decisive action, there will be a long wait for a healthier environment" (p. 148)

(2) influencing the end state: "We should not rely on financial markets to give us a properly sized defense industrial base" (p. 148).

Third, Norman Augustine, CEO of Martin Marietta in 1993, provided a defense industry view. "Survival demands that companies combine with former competitors and mutate into new species." And "it's better to have two or three healthy companies than fifteen weak companies under any scenario" (Augustine, 1997).

All three noted the importance of astute leadership by the government. This included dependable planning guidance for the industrial base, especially regulatory reviews: "antitrust laws or, more precisely, the process of *applying* antitrust laws, creates uncertainty" (Augustine, 1997). "My only hope would be that the government would make up its mind and tell industry what it wants and stick with it" (Augustine, quoted in Aitoro, 2016).

## 5.7 Acquisition Reform Initiatives in the 1990s

The DoD also embarked on acquisition reform measures in the 1990s, viewed as complementary to industrial base consolidation and efficiency. These included the following: simplification of purchases; increased reliance on commercial standards as opposed to military specifications; making DoD acquisition practices similar to commercial activity; and updating DoD acquisition rules, and more fully publicizing defense business opportunities (Fox *et al.*, 2011, pp. - 151–180).

Assessments of these reforms' outcomes are provided by Reig (2000) and Fox *et al.* (2011), among others. Reig (2000) offered generally favorable assessments (pp. 34–40), while Fox *et al.* (2011) was less impressed with the long-term outcomes (pp. 151–188), stating that systemic incentives remained largely unchanged (pp. 180–188). "Reluctance to establish more appropriate incentives has been a serious deficiency in most DoD improvement programs during the past five decades" Fox *et al.* (2011, p. 204).

In any case, some parts of the program did not go as planned. Deutch (2001, p. 142) noted that the intended sharing of cost savings with the industrial base did not occur. Also, the sudden merger turnabout in the 1998 disapproval of the LM–NG merger caused considerable uncertainty. "The absence of a clear signal ending the consolidation policy is unfortunate because it left several defense firms 'stranded on a different course'" (Deutch, 2001, p. 138).

## 5.8 Means to Preserve Competition

The government has means to review the effects of the proposed consolidations on competition. In particular, the Department of Justice (DOJ), the FTC, and the DoD are empowered and mandated to conduct such reviews. In this case of defense industrial consolidation, the DoD's Office of the General Counsel conducts reviews in conjunction with the FTC, DOJ, or both (Office of the General Counsel Department of Defense, 2017).

The DoD's General Counsel has a broad remit to review proposed consolidations relevant to covered transactions. Specifics appear in section 2 of DoD Directive 5000.62 (2017). Reviews can involve virtually any DoD agency, for a wide variety of open-ended reasons (Office of the General Counsel Department of Defense, 2017, esp. para. 1.2, p. 1). Covered-transaction reviews are mandated for a wide variety of reasons – including, "(a)ny other aspect of the covered transaction that might impact DoD access to affordable or innovative sources to include … essential data rights" (Office of the General Counsel Department of Defense, 2017, para. 1.2.1[7], p. 3). These powers and responsibilities have been in place for some time. GAO testimony to Congress in 1998 contains a good summary of remedies available to the government (Cooper, 1998) and the government can disapprove the proposal (e.g., Lockheed–Martin with NG in 1998).

Short of that, the government can direct actions to remediate the undesirable effects of the transaction: (1) divestment of corporate divisions to prevent consolidation in particular market segments (e.g., UTC's acquisition of Rockwell Collins in 2018); and (2) various forms of "consent decrees" that specify actions to be taken to remediate anticompetitive effects (e.g., NG's acquisition of Orbital–ATK in 2018). One form of consent decree is agreeing to a "firewall," "intended to limit or prevent the exchange of competition sensitive information among parts of the company" (Cooper, 1998, p. 3).[41]

### 5.8.1 Observed Effects on Competition

The number of suppliers as a metric for competition is deeply embedded in standard economics. Principles texts classify market types by number of suppliers, along with product differentiation. A related concept is market concentration quantified, for example, by the Herfindahl-Hirschman Index, which the US DOJ considers a useful benchmark for antitrust inquiries (DOJ, 2018).

---

[41] A specific firewall consent decree is discussed as part of the earlier GBSD case.

By such measures, there has clearly been a reduction in competition. A GAO Congressional testimony reported a significant decrease in first-tier suppliers in a number of defense industrial market segments (Cooper, 1998, pp. 6–8).

In a National Bureau of Economic Research (NBER) study, Carril and Duggan (2018) set out to study the implications of market structure and public-sector acquisition outcomes (p. 1). As a natural experiment, they chose to study defense industry consolidation (1985–2001, p. 2). They found fewer firms in the market and a greater concentration, with a greater share of DoD contract revenue going to the five largest firms (esp., pp. 2, 44). In addition, "increased market concentration *caused* the procurement process to become less competitive," finding robust empirical support for the conclusion (emphasis added, p. 22). Carril and Duggan (2018) also found a significantly increased percentage of source selections with one bid (p. 2), a movement toward cost-plus contracts and away from fixed-price contracts (p. 3).

The GAO Weapon System Annual Assessment published in 2019 (US Government Accountability Office, 2019) reached similar conclusions:

- "DOD MDAPs operate in an environment of limited competition and a constrained defense contractor base" (p. 35); and
- "A small group of contractors received the majority of major contract award dollars" (US Government Accountability Office, 2019, p. 40).

In the aftermath of the Last Supper, Kovacic and Smallwood (1994) provided a very interesting, view of the state of competition for aerial systems. These are summarized in Table 6.

**Table 6** State of competition for aerial systems in 1994

| Companies | Capabilities | | | | |
|---|---|---|---|---|---|
| | Carrier-based | Stealthy | Commercial | "Market share" | "Avionics" |
| Boeing | | | × | | × |
| Grumman | × | | | × | × |
| Lockheed | | × | | × | |
| McDonnell Douglas | × | | × | × | |
| Northrop | | × | | | |
| Total firms | 2 | 2 | 2 | 3 | 2 |

**Notes:** "Market share" refers to serial production of combat aircraft. Northrop is not credited with this capability despite its B-2 program – apparently because of its low production rate and much shortened production run.
**Source:** Kovacic and Smallwood (1994).

The authors then analyzed possible mergers with respect to preserving DoD choices for future aircraft systems. An extrapolation and update of their analysis appears in Table 7.

It's worth noting that actual consolidation in this part of the defense industry preserved rivalries in every capability except production of commercial aircraft – also military tanker and transport aircraft. Continuation of a commercial airframe rivalry was unlikely in any case. In the 1990s, it became evident that McDonnell Douglas could no longer compete with Boeing and Airbus airliners. So, from a competition-preserving perspective, consolidation in the aircraft segment went reasonably well in the 1990s. A look at the current situation is also informative.

## 5.9 Defense Industry Consolidation: A 2020 Perspective

A postscript (2020) on the defense marketplace appears in Table 8. Again, we borrow from Kovacic and Smallwood (1994), however, we revise the capabilities of interest to accord with changes in military affairs and the threat environment: changing "avionics" to "systems integration," reflecting increased complexity of military systems. Unmanned aerial systems (UASs) have become an increasingly important part of air combat, and we add UASs as a capability of interest. Finally, "network centric military operations are increasingly important with advances in technology" (Schaefer, 2020). This is reflected in the network integration (NWI) capability.

A mixed picture emerges, with considerable consolidation resulting in fewer suppliers, especially in the traditional platform sectors. As noted, this has led to more single-bid contract negotiations, most dramatically in the case of GBSD. Also, one Army RFP for a new armored fighting vehicle (AFV) resulted in only one response, which did not meet the Army specifications (Stone, 2020). More generally, the DoD's DIB assessment for 2018 reported a significant number of capabilities in important areas of the defense supply chain residing in single firms (U.S. Department of Defense, 2019).

On the other hand, changes in military affairs put new emphasis on IT and increased the importance of shared situational awareness in combat forces. Part of this is an increased importance of space assets as information-gathering nodes. In these areas, new entrants into the defense market, actual and potential, are predominantly commercial firms such as Microsoft and Amazon. The ongoing JEDI melodrama illustrates tech giants' high degree of interest in doing business with the DoD, potentially broadening the DIB.

Consolidation does not necessarily have irreversible effects on the number of firms in the various market segments. For example, Boeing is still a potential

**Table 7** Major defense companies' capabilities to produce aerial combat systems (late 1990s perspective)

| Companies | Capabilities | | | | |
|---|---|---|---|---|---|
| | Carrier-based | Stealthy | Commercial | "Market share" | "Avionics" |
| Boeing | × | | × | × | × |
| NG | × | × | | × | × |
| Lockheed–Martin | | × | | × | |
| Total firms | 2 | 2 | 1 | 3 | 2 |

**Source:** Extrapolated from Kovacic and Smallwood (1994), authors' judgments

**Table 8** View of air combat industrial capabilities: A 2020 perspective

| Companies | Capabilities | | | | | | |
|---|---|---|---|---|---|---|---|
| | Carrier air | Stealthy | Communications | Combat | Systems integration | UASs | NWI |
| Boeing | × | [a] | × | × | × | × | |
| LM | × | × | | × | × | × | |
| NG | | × | [b] | ×[c] | × | × | |
| General atomics & others *et al.* | | | | | | × | |
| Info tech companies* | | | | | | | × |
| Total firms | 2 | 2+ | 1+ | 3 | 3 | 4[d] | Many[e] |

**Notes:** [a] Boeing is a potential source of stealthy airframes, as a major player in the Joint Advanced Strike Techology (JAST) then Joint Striker (JSF) program. It was also part of a team (with LM) that submitted a proposal for the B-21 program. [b] Airbus, perhaps partnered with NG or LM, is still a potential supplier of military aircraft adapted from commercial designs. [c] NG was added to the "combat" capability list because of the ongoing B-21 program. [d] Four major UAS suppliers (Peck, 2016). [e] Six firms expressed interest in JEDI, 44 in ABMS (not all as potential prime contractors).

*Source:* Extrapolated from Kovacic and Smallwood (1994), authors' judgments

supplier of stealthy aircraft, increasing market contestability. Likewise, a firm like NG or Lockheed–Martin could offer military systems based on commercial airframes in conjunction with, say, Airbus. Worth noting also is that the most competitive defense markets, such as UASs and NWI, feature firms that are primarily commercial.

### 5.9.1 Effects on DoD Costs

Given the reduction in the number of suppliers in the various defense market sectors, one would expect an increase in suppliers' market power and increases in costs. However, not all analyses support this supposition. GAO Congressional testimony (Cooper, 1998) concerning the defense marketplace in the wake of the large-scale consolidation in the 1990s indicates "there is little evidence that the increased consolidation has adversely affected current programs." Cooper hypothesized that antitrust reviews of proposed consolidations had identified and remediated adverse effects of reduced competition (Cooper 1998, esp. pp. 1, 2).

Another GAO publication in 1998 found cost savings from a set of seven specific defense industry consolidations but reported being unable to sort out the effects of reorganization from other things, such as quantity changes and manufacturing process improvements (Cooper, 1998, esp. pp. 2, 6).

Hensel (2010) reviewed defense industry consolidation for the previous two decades. Her basic conclusion was "Somewhat more systems were likely to exhibit lower post-merger ... unit costs." Noting that "evidence suggested greater efficiencies following consolidation for many sectors." In short, Hensel (2010) views the consolidation movement as generally successful from a DoD perspective.

The Carril and Duggan (2018) study cited earlier reached a similar conclusion, "we find no evidence that consolidation led to a significant increase in acquisition costs of large weapon systems, nor to increased spending at the product market level" (p. 3). "If anything, our results suggest the opposite" (Carril and Duggan, 2018, p. 24), and market segments with greater concentration did not experience a higher increase in cost (Carril and Duggan, 2018, p. 27).

The authors hypothesize that monopsony buying power can negate the expected effects of greater market concentration (Carril and Duggan, 2018, p. 28). More specifically, two factors in the defense marketplace that increase prices are (1) the attendant shift away from fixed-price contracts, and (2) more market power accruing to suppliers, which enable negotiation of higher markups (p. 28). Countering these effects are (1) higher efficiencies from consolidation in shrinking markets, and (2) government's market power as a monopsonist (Carril and Duggan, 2018,

p. 28). The authors offer these two sets of effects as largely offsetting each other. Kovacic and Smallwood (1994, p. 101) concur.

These are interesting results and suggest two broader observations. First, the commonly understood characteristics of standard markets do not necessarily apply to markets with sovereign monopsonists. Second, there is no guarantee that these two sets of market forces (fewer suppliers versus monopsony power) will continue to offset each other.

### 5.9.2 Effects on Innovation

Perry's list of likely failures includes lack of innovation. A long-standing microeconomic orthodoxy is that monopolies do little innovating. As Sir John Hicks put it: "The best of all monopoly profits is a quiet life" (Hicks, 1935). On the other hand, prospects for monopoly profits are conducive to innovation (Solow, 2003, p. 2), noting that Schumpeter posed the question of the relationship between degree of competition and innovative activity "long ago" (p. 3).

More recently, Aghion (2003) and others have taken up the question, "Theoretical IO literature predicts that innovation and growth should decline with competition. On the other hand, empirical work has pointed out a positive correlation between product market competition and innovative output" (Aghion, 2003, p. 142). Aghion's answer is (basically) that innovative activity is not a monotonic function of market competition but rather reaches a maximum at some number of suppliers in the market (Aghion, 2003, pp. 156–165).

This clearly indicates that significant innovation activities can occur in oligopolistic markets. Baumol (2002) states that strong innovation "arms races" can occur among a rather small group of suppliers featuring "oligopolistic rivalry and continuous innovation spending" (Baumol, 2002, pp. 43–54). His results strongly suggest that "oligopoly firms routinize . . . the entire innovation process" (pp. 53–54).

A recent example of innovation in oligopolies comes from the unfriendly rivalry between Airbus and Boeing in airliners. Around 2010, Boeing decided not to replace its 737 family of airliners until the early 2020s (Freed, 2011). Being too slow to innovate can be a prelude to disaster – as the Boeing 737 MAX case demonstrates (Pickar and Franck, 2021).[42] In short, fewer firms need not lessen innovation, but can increase it, since falling behind can be very costly.

---

[42] There was a number of causes for the 737 MAX program failure. Pickar and Franck (2021) trace these back to 2010, when Boeing chose not to start work on a 737 replacement. As a result, Boeing was caught flat-footed by the reengined Airbus 320 family – which led to something of a forced-march development program for Boeing. This, in turn, led to a 737 MAX design with flawed flight-control software. The Federal Aviation Administration could have stepped in at

## 5.10 Consolidation as a Consequence of DoD Acquisition Practices

Whatever the results of the post-1993 consolidations, part of the cause is the DoD itself. There was active encouragement of mergers (1993–1998). More recently, there is a strong tendency for major defense acquisitions to be structured as long-term, high-value, winner-takes-all programs. Among the vocal supporters of the winner-takes-all approach was Secretary Robert M. Gates: "make sure there is competition for contracts, but real competition, not the kind Congress likes where everybody wins (such as proposals on the Hill to split the tanker buy between Boeing and Airbus)" (Gates, 2014, p. 459).

The lesson for contemporary defense industrial firms is clear. Those without multiple business lines can be one losing proposal away from corporate death. On the other hand, firms with diversified operations deal with such setbacks with much less difficulty. Thus, for example, shortly after withdrawing from the new ICBM (GBSD) competition, Boeing was reported to be "moving on … Employees working on the project are being reassigned to other projects within the company" (Weisgerber, 2019). Similarly, NG, which recently cancelled its OmegA heavy SLV, still has substantial work in the same general market segment: SLV boosters (Erwin, 2020a) and the new ICBM (GBSD; Cohen, 2020).

## 6 Limits on Sovereign Monopsony

Even though the government is a sovereign monopsonist, its reign is not absolute. First, the US government is not a unitary whole. It consists of separate and sometimes contentious parts inherent in its separation-of-powers structure. Franck and Udis (2017), for example, concluded that the government sometimes functions more like a "quarrelsome committee" than the monopsonist in standard economic theory. The KC-X source selection processes were cited as a good example. At times, Boeing and the Airbus Group exploited the committee's quarrels, and appeared to have veto power over the process at times (Franck, Lewis, and Udis, 2008, esp. pp. 2, 36).

Second, there has been a long-term decrease in the number of first-tier contractors. As one observer put it, "Power has shifted from the Defense Department to the defense contractors. The Pentagon has less leverage when there are fewer places to go" (Wayne, 1998b).

Third, the power balance changes after source selection – the "fundamental transformation" defined in transaction cost economics literature (e.g., Williamson, 1996, esp. pp. 13, 16, 178). The winning firm becomes the sole

---

some point but the regulators ability to understand the software problems would have been difficult (if not impossible) because Boeing likewise didn't understand them.

supplier for products such as the F-35. This results in a bilateral monopoly consistent with the model summarized in Greenfield and Brady (2008, p. 66). The annual bargaining ritual between the DoD and Lockheed–Martin for F-35 prices is a good example. As a sovereign monopsonist, however, the DoD can dictate a price, as in Production Lot 9 (Clark, 2016).

A fourth limit to government power is bid protests, which are intended to provide self-interested enforcement of competitive norms through challenges to procurement decisions. Bid protests, or the possibility, can increase defense firms' bargaining power relative to the DoD.

Finally, sovereign monopsony includes burdens. For example, the government must take some responsibility for the management and welfare of its suppliers. The DoD's management of the industrial base for heavy SLVs is a case in point.

The satellite market is becoming bifurcated. Small satellites, on average, are getting lighter (Kosiak, 2019, pp. 7–8; Triezenberg *et al.*, 2020, esp. pp. 2–3) and large satellites are getting more massive. Also, the distinction between heavy SLVs and interplanetary launchers is decreasing (Triezenberg *et al.*, 2020, p. 3). Among other things, this means that the market for launch services for those larger satellites is becoming more distinct.

Heavy launch satellite vehicle suppliers have two main market segments for sales: government (national security satellites (NSSs), and other government agencies), and commercial (Chaplain, 2016, pp. 1–2; Triezenberg *et al.*, 2020, p. 5). However, firms cannot participate in the entire market, for a variety of reasons. Many governments, like the US, restrict NSS launches to domestic firms. Some launch services are acquired as part of vertical integration – for example, the entire launch package: rockets plus satellites, also self-provisioned launches.

What is open to all or most SLV suppliers has been termed "addressable" (Triezenberg *et al.*, 2020, pp. 11–12). It is a relatively small part of the entire launch vehicle market, about 20 launches per year (Triezenberg *et al.*, 2020, p. 20), about a third of the total. Since the commercial segment is generally accessible, foreign suppliers affect prospects for US suppliers (Triezenberg *et al.*, 2020, p. 27). Likewise, US corporate strategies affect the domestic heavy lift industrial base: "The number of US firms that can be supported by the demand in the launch markets will be dependent on the strategic choices of these firms (Triezenberg *et al.*, 2020, p. 29).

The US heavy launch vehicle enterprise is in a period of transition. Previously, the United Launch Alliance's (ULA's)[43] SLVs, Atlas V and Delta IV, are modified and upgraded variants of the Atlas ICBM and Thor IRBM.

---

[43] A joint venture of Boeing and Lockheed–Martin.

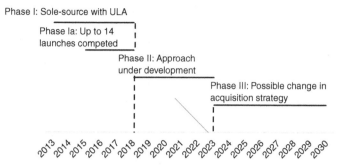

**Figure 12** Timeline of introduction of competition into heavy national security
space launches
**Sources:** Triezenberg *et al.* (2020, p. 20); US Government Accountability Office (2015, p. 7)

Both were developed in the 1950s and retired from their nuclear strike roles in
the 1960s. They are regarded as approaching the end of their useful lives.

From 2005 to 2016, the ULA was essentially a monopoly for heavy-lift NSS
launches (Boeing, 2020). Four heavy lift replacements are now in development
to replace the current SLVs that have been in service for a long time, and past
experience strongly indicates that they likely would not be ready for operational
missions by their current estimated dates.

A further complication was that the Atlas V had been modified with the RD-180,
an excellent Russian rocket motor. With the Russian invasion of the Ukraine in
2014, Congress mandated RD-180 phaseout (Petersen, 2014). This meant a new
motor or retirement for the Atlas V. ULA chose Blue Origin's BE-4. But the BE-4
has experienced significant delays (Berger, 2021).[44]

But a more significant disruption to ULA's quiet life[45] was competition.
SpaceX had considerable success against ULA: winning 15 of the 24 NSS
and NASA launches as of March 2020 (Burghardt, 2020) – in Phase Ia of the Air
Force heavy SLV plan (shown in Figure 12). This, as one would expect, added
impetus to ULA's development of its new Vulcan heavy launch system.

## 6.1 Air Force Management of the Heavy SLV Industrial Base

The Air Force is the DoD executive agency (10 US Code Section 2273) for
acquiring SLVs. Accordingly, the Air Force was obliged to formulate a plan for

---

[44] This is interesting because and extended-life Atlas V is a potential hedge against the risk of major
availability delays in the Vulcan.
[45] A much-quoted statement from Sir John Hicks is "The greatest monopoly profit is a quiet life"
(Hicks, 1935).

**Table 9** State of US NSS heavy SLVs prior to Phase II selection

| Satellite launch vehicle | Supplier | Operational |
|---|---|---|
| Atlas V | ULA[a] | 2002 |
| Delta IV | ULA | 2007 |
| Falcon Heavy | Space X | 2018 |
| Vulcan | ULA | 2020/1[b,c] |
| OmegA | NG | 2021/2[b] |
| New Glenn | Blue Origin | 2021/4[b] |

**Notes:** [a] ULA, a Lockheed–Martin–Boeing joint venture. [b] In development. First flight estimated at 202X/Y (Yth quarter of 202X). OmegA cancelled in 2020 after Phase II downselect. [c] Vulcan initial launch was estimated for "early 2021"[46] (Neal, 2020). Neal regarded this as optimistic.

launch vehicles suitable for heavy NSSs. The Air Force is also mandated to ensure the health of the heavy SLV industrial base (also in Section 2273).

Heavy US SLVs (operational or in development) relevant to Phase II are shown in Table 9. The plan itself was published in 2015, in three phases, as shown in Figure 12. At Phase II, starting in 2018, the Air Force would provide launch service contracts for two SLV suppliers. It received pushback from concerned industrial firms (Berger, 2019) and Congress, with US GAO (2015), expressing doubts based on oversight (pp. 8–13) and risk (pp. 19–21). One result of the controversy was the Air Force tasking the RAND Corporation to assess the implications of the Air Force plan, and to report findings and recommendations as appropriate.

### 6.1.1 US Firms Contending for Phase II Air Force Support

In 2018, the DoD provided launch development support to three firms: ULA, NG, and Blue Origin (Erwin, 2018b) – with the SpaceX's heavy lift launcher (Falcon Heavy) already operational.

### 6.1.2 The RAND SLV Study

The RAND tasking from the Air Force Space and Missile Systems Center was translated to two major questions: (Triezenberg *et al.*, 2020, esp. pp. iii, xi, xii).

(1) What are the potential impacts of near-term Air Force SLV acquisition decisions on assured access to space and the ability to sustain two domestic firms in the heavy-lift SLV market over the next 10 years?

---

[46] Now rescheduled for 2022.

(2) How many US providers will the SLV market sustain over the long term?

Given that best the DoD depends at least in part on US SLV providers' corporate strategy, the RAND analysis identified four business strategies for SLV providers:

(1) commercial only;
(2) national security, plus commercial;
(3) US NSS and other US "nonaddressable" launch opportunities
(4) a diversified portfolio of products to service US national security, other US nonaddressable opportunities, and smaller satellite launch opportunities.

Companies committed to a commercial-only strategy are not a matter of direct interest. However, they can have an indirect effect on the NSS segment by competing for commercial launches with NSS providers.

Clearly a SLV supplier who successfully executes a diversified strategy (NSS plus commercial) needs less NSS launch business than one who competes only for defense and other government satellite launches.

### 6.1.2.1 RAND's Conclusions and Recommendation

Major conclusions:

(1) Competition for commercial launch vehicles will intensify with the proliferation of international capabilities to support heavy satellite launches. Some consolidation among US firms is highly likely.
(2) Using assured access to space as a primary benchmark, the Air Force heavy-lift SLV plan entails significant risks with respect to assured access to space in the near term, through 2023. The nature of the risk is depicted nicely on page 54 of Triezenberg *et al.* (2020). Factors leading to risk include the following (Triezenberg *et al.*, 2020, pp. 68–69):
    (a) launch schedule perturbations, "demand slips";
    (b) increased costs if NSS providers are not successful in the commercial launch market;
    (c) development delays for new SLVs, Vulcan, OmegA, and New Glenn;
    (d) less-than-expected access to legacy SLVs.
(3) The US heavy-lift launcher market is unlikely to support more than two firms over an extended period (Triezenberg *et al.*, 2020, pp. 45–46). This implies significant consolidations among heavy launch vehicles should be expected.[47]

---

[47] However, it is interesting to note that recent entrants (SpaceX and Blue Origin) have placed significant bets on the emergence of a market with room for more suppliers.

Supporting an interim third provider would allow more time for market forces to sort out the details of consolidation by removing the government from picking winners among launch vehicle providers (Triezenberg *et al.*, 2020, p. 70). It might also discourage non-US providers from entering the commercial satellite market (Triezenberg *et al.*, 2020, pp. 54, 63).

The main recommendation was to seriously consider risk-mitigation measures for the near term (Triezenberg *et al.*, 2020, p. 70). Other recommendations include:

(1) supporting a third launch provider during Phase II until 2024;
(2) negotiating (and paying for) priority access to legacy launchers for the near term (Triezenberg *et al.*, 2020, p. 54, fig. 5.5).

On August 7, the Air Force awarded its Phase II contracts to ULA and SpaceX for FY 2022–2027 (US Department of Defense, 2020a). Despite the RAND recommendations regarding risk reduction concerns over both risk and oversight in Phase II (GAO, 2015; Triezenberg *et al.*, 2020), the Air Force awarded the entire launch group to those two companies. On September 9, NG ceased development of its OmegA SLV (Erwin, 2020b).

This is a situation in which the monopsonist (the DoD) deals with firms that have other opportunities, which include the commercial market and other government agencies. Policy deliberations become accordingly more complicated, and the sovereign monopsonist's burden accordingly heavier.

This example also highlights the role of research and analysis organizations like RAND and the GAO. They can, and frequently do, have significant roles in the operations of the US defense economy. However, their views do not always prevail.

## 6.2 Bid Protests: Another Limit

The bid protest system's foundation is the Competition in Contracting Act (CICA) of 1984. The stated rationale for bid protests is to lessen the risk of fraud and the effects of error in federal government procurement and to increase competition. Bid protests enable a decentralized network of self-interested, informed overseers to ensure that the procurement process operates consistently with competitive norms, thus, encouraging prospective vendors to compete for defense business (Melese, 2018, p. 669).

There are some reasons to believe that the protest system works reasonably well. A RAND study (Arena *et al.*, 2018, esp. pp. xvii–xviii) reported that protests have the following characteristics:

(1) are generally viewed favorably by contractors and unfavorably by government officials;

(2) are relatively uncommon, but increasing in recent years;

(3) are unlikely to be filed without merit; and

(4) have a declining appeals rate if unsuccessful.

The report recommended some adjustments to the current system, such as emphasizing the quality of debriefings to unsuccessful bidders.

A US GAO report on protests filed with the agency in FY 2019 reported that 13% of protests were sustained, generally due to errors or inadequacies in the source selection. Also that the affected agencies undertook corrective actions on their own to settle a significant fraction of protests (Armstrong, 2019, pp. 2, 5).

Bid protests have disadvantages. First is the possibility of structuring source selections to avoid protests. One approach is to simplify the selection criteria, perhaps to something like lowest price technically acceptable (LPTA), which is relatively easy to defend against a protest. (JEDI, discussed later, is an example of why program managers are motivated to avoid bid protests.)

The Air Force structured the final KC-X source selection, in 2011, for example, according to a variation of LPTA. Phase I was an assessment of 372 tests, with passing assessments for all of them needed to be technically acceptable. The next step involved total proposed price (TPP) modified with analyses of operational effectiveness, life-cycle fuel expense, and associated construction costs, which lead to a total evaluated price (TEP). If the TEPs were very close, the Air Force used a tie breaker, a scoring of nice-to-have features (Franck, Lewis, and Udis, 2012, pp. 14–16).

Under Secretary of Defense Lynn offered a revealing assessment, "We think we've established a clear, a transparent and an open process. We think we've executed on that, and that will not yield grounds for protest" (US Department of Defense, 2011).

Second, protests and their resolution can extract transaction costs associated with stop-work orders and delays in programs. Also, bidders can threaten a protest, with the intent of influencing the competition itself or extracting some advantages from risk-averse or hurried program managers. Melese (2018, p. 670) called this practice "fedmail."

### 6.2.1 The JEDI Cloud Program

The DoD's JEDI Cloud is intended to provide data services throughout the defense establishment (US Department of Defense, 2020a), with a system adapted from existing commercial alternatives. The JEDI Cloud is regarded as especially important to rapid and informed decision-making by US operational commands (Peters, 2019a, p. 5).

Like KC-X, there were multiple experienced and competent potential suppliers. These included Amazon, Google, IBM, Microsoft, Oracle and REAN. What could have been a quick, clean source selection became messy and prolonged.

### 6.2.1.1 Acquiring JEDI

This has not been a smooth road ... contract protests, internal investigations and conflict-of-interest allegations that have bedeviled the source selection. (Eversden, 2019)

... a mind-bending legal matter. (Freedberg Jr., 2019)

The original memo outlining the JEDI program was published in September 2017 (Peters, 2019a, summary). A first draft of the RFP appeared in March 2018, with the RFP process complete in October 2018 (Peters, 2019a, p. 7). In October 2018, Google withdrew, citing possible incompatibility with corporate values, specifications outside its core competencies, and the winner-takes-all nature of the process (Chan, 2018). At this point, Amazon was considered the favorite (Chan, 2018).

In November, Oracle protested to the GAO regarding conflicts of interest with Amazon employees, past and future, involved in the JEDI program. The GAO did not sustain the protest, per a decision in December (Peters, 2019b, p. 1). Subsequently, Oracle took its case to federal court, but got another unfavorable ruling in July 2019 (Peters, 2019b, p. 1).

In April 2019, the DoD down-selected from four proposals to two finalists: Amazon and Microsoft (Peters, 2019a, summary, p. 7). In July 2019, President Trump ordered a secretary of defense review of the JEDI source selection process (Nickelsburg, 2019; Selyukh, 2019).

In October 2019, the DoD announced the JEDI contract award to Microsoft (McKinnon and Tilley, 2019; Peters, 2019b). Amazon protested the award through a complaint lodged in federal court that alleged: (1) improper political interference in the process[48] and (2) that Amazon's proposal thoroughly outclassed Microsoft's (Freedberg Jr., 2020; Peters, 2019b; Shepardson, 2020).[49]

---

[48] President Trump was reported to have expressed a desire to "screw Amazon" in the Summer of 2018 (Nickelsburg, 2019).

[49] Not all assessments agreed with Amazon's. Some concluded that Microsoft had progressed a great deal in its ability to deliver a workable JEDI Cloud to the DoD (Freedberg Jr., 2019; Peters, 2019b, p. 1).

In February 2020, a federal judge levied an injunction to stop work on JEDI, one day prior to contractor start, on the grounds that Amazon's claims had merit (Serbu, 2020). In April, the court approved a motion to remand the matter to the DoD, which would review its handling of parts of the selection process (Freedberg Jr., 2020). Amazon was opposed to this measure and continued its litigation over various parts of the RFP (Serbu, 2020).

### 6.2.1.2 JEDI in 2021

As of this writing, JEDI is still a mind-bending legal matter. The JEDI program was put on hold into 2021. The DoD, with its remand from a federal judge, reevaluated the Amazon and Microsoft proposals and chose Microsoft, again, in September (Wilkers, 2020). Amazon continued to protest. With various possibilities for legal maneuver and judicial determination, the process continues.

This melodrama is indeed far from over and this JEDI effort may not be salvageable. As one experienced DoD official put it: "because the . . . program is suffering so many delays while technology forges ahead, it is being litigated into irrelevance" (Freedberg Jr., 2020), rather like the Jarndyce and Jarndyce case from Victorian fiction.[50] The DoD has indeed indicated willingness to abandon JEDI (at least this iteration) if litigation turns out to be prolonged – despite there being an "urgent, unmet requirement" (US Department of Defense, 2021).

The bid protest has affected the acquisition process in unintended way, including conduct of source selection notifications. For sufficiently valuable contract awards, the program office is required to provide a debriefing to unsuccessful bidders regarding the rationale for the contract decision. That briefing may be oral or written. According to DoD source selection procedures, one major purpose of the debriefing is to discourage bid protests (US Department of Defense Office of the Inspector General, 2020, p. 80).

This has caused some degree of controversy regarding best practice for such briefings. There are at least two issues. Should the briefing be written or oral (Asch, 2020; Field, 2017, p. 8)? Also, should the briefer emphasize transparency or limit the discussion to the minimum information required (Asch, 2020; Field, 2017, pp. 4–5)? Regardless of the merits of these positions, it is clear that the possibility of a protest has introduced an adversarial element in source selection debriefings (Asch, 2020).

Overall, a mixed picture emerges regarding the usefulness of bid protests. Schwartz and Manuel (2015), among others, characterize the issues well.

---

[50] The case appears in Charles Dickens's novel *Bleak House* concerning the distribution of a large estate. Lengthy litigation eventually dissipated all of the assets in the dispute. In short, the estate was litigated into irrelevance (Sensagent, 2020).

## 6.3 Emerging Developments in a Time of Rapid Change

We have provided an overview of the US defense economy, aiming to convey its characteristics and peculiarities. Some main themes we note here are:

(1) the US defense economy has many important institutional peculiarities;
(2) the US defense economy is evolving for a number of reasons:
    (a) the continuing consolidation of the long-standing defense industrial incumbents;
    (b) rapid advance of military applications of IT;
    (c) new entries to the DIB – especially in NWI and unmanned systems.

However, one feature worth further emphasis is that military-technical advances and the state of military affairs are both rapidly changing. Hence, we conclude with our view of significant future developments.

First, however, is a disclaimer; namely "prediction is very difficult, especially about the future."[51] A confident prediction from the 1990s held that large defense firms would have more commercial business in their portfolios. Lockheed–Martin, for example, would have only 25% of its revenue from defense by 2010 (Wayne, 1998a). However, the defense percentage of Lockheed–Martin revenue increased from 64% in 1998 to 93% in 2010, and 95% in 2019 (*DefenseNews*, 2019).

With that in mind, we humbly offer some thoughts about forces of change in the US defense economy, supported by some significant and promising developments currently underway. We believe many of them will survive the perils that afflict all innovations, including institutional reluctance and resource scarcity.

### 6.3.1 Emerging Trends in Military Affairs

#### 6.3.1.1 Managing a Difficult Era of "Defense Against What?"

When Hitch, McKean, and Enke (1960) posed the "defense against what" question, the answers were relatively simple (pp. 7–14). The primary threat was the Soviet Union. There were two important planning contingencies – nuclear and conventional – occurring in three "domains" for combat operations: land, sea, and air.

Toward the end of the Cold War, not much changed, although insurgent and proxy wars (theirs and ours) became more common. Space was still a relatively permissive environment.

---

[51] Attributed to Neils Bohr, and others.

Now, there are more threats: great powers, regional powers, and non-state actors (*The Dragons and the Snakes*; Kilcullen, 2020, esp. chap. 1). There are also more domains for military action plus a significant expansion of methods to wage war.

The new domains include information warfare, electronic warfare,[52] disinformation operations, cyber-attack, and space combat operations. Operating effectively in multiple domains simultaneously is now regarded as an important military capability (The White House, 2017, p. 28). The pace, breadth, and impact of current military-technical advances are remarkable.

Perhaps even more important is the increasing use of military action intended to avoid a large-scale military response. Proxy combatants have complicated military affairs. Examples include Russian troops employed in seizing the Crimea (2014) and Iran's long-standing cooperation with Hezbollah (Kilcullen, 2020, pp. 102, 109, 221).

This complicated, changing, and dangerous defense environment will likely shape the defense economy for the foreseeable future.

## 6.3.1.2 Major Military-Technical Advances

Our view of the most likely technical developments over the next few decades, and a partial view of their potential, is summarized in Figure 13. The operational tasks associated with high-intensity, network-centric warfare are shown in Figure 13a. The main technical enablers of military capability improvements in this conflict realm are shown in Figure 13a. The basic combat tasks are connected with dashed lines. The "technical enablers" are components and subsystems sufficiently well developed to be included in combat systems. These in general have a technology readiness level (TRL) of about 7.[53]

Figure 13b offers underlying technologies that can become the "technical enablers" of increased operational capability. These are developing technologies with lower levels of technical readiness.

Our observations are, first, a large of number of very promising technologies will find military applications – and will likely change the military environment significantly. Second, IT remains a foundation for military-technical innovation

---

[52] As noted, electronic warfare was traditionally used for tactical support. It is now deemed capable of effecting disruptions at the operational and strategic levels.

[53] Basically, "(t)echnology Readiness Levels (TRLs) are a method for assessing the technical maturity of a technology during its acquisition phase" (TWI Global, 2021). TRL7 indicates technologies demonstrated and tested (but not fully) and are "near or at" a maturity sufficient for deployment as an operational system (US Government Accountability Office, 2016, esp. p7).

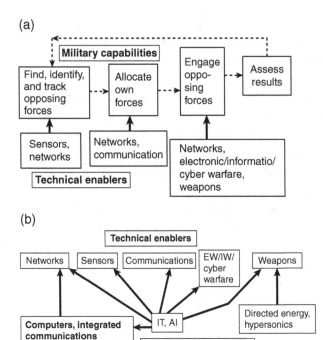

**Figure 13** (a) Technology advances affecting military capabilities (a partial view); (b) underlying technical advances

**Note:** Underlying technologies provide the foundation for the technical enablers, as indicated by the arrows.

**Sources:** Extrapolated from Future of Defense Task Force (2020); O'Hanlon (2018), authors' judgments

(as Figure 13b implies). Third, these developments are interrelated. Accordingly, funding and managing defense research and development looks to be a complex task.

### 6.3.1.3 Increasing Importance of Human Capital in Combat Forces

Advances in military technology will lead to greater importance for military human capital. First, technology-related billets in the armed forces will (as a primary operational need) be added, particularly in IT fields (e.g., Warwick, 2016).

Second, the reconnaissance-strike mode of warfare, with its potential for both destruction of assets and disruption of operations, will dictate (1) greater speed of combat operations (Freeman and Lyons, 2020), and (2) greater resilience in disrupted operational environments. This means improved decision-making abilities at lower levels of combat operations – including more human capital (Eckstein, 2020).

Third, future high-intensity combat operations mean more dispersed operations with smaller units. That, in turn, means future soldiers must be less specialized – that is, each individual must have more than one skill (Everstine, 2021). Individuals proficient in more skills means more training, and more human capital formation.

The US military has taken notice. For example, Space Force is developing a human capital strategy (Erwin, 2021). Also, the Air Force has undertaken initiatives to systematically track its human capital stock (Serbu, 2016).

### 6.3.1.3.1Example: Artificial Intelligence

Although regarded as a revolutionary change in the conduct of war, introduction of artificial intelligence (AI) in the "kill chain" is no panacea for military decision-making.

One reason is that algorithms used to "train" AI systems are not perfect. This can lead to misperceptions in AI-based situation assessments, with corresponding possibilities for very costly consequences. Avoiding or mitigating them "will depend on the operator's education and training in the relevant technology" (Chapa, 2021).

At the strategic level, "(t)he artificial intelligence (AI) competition will not be won by the side with the best technology. It will be won by the side with the best, most diverse and tech-savvy talent" (National Security Commission on Artificial Intelligence, 2021, p. 59) – that is, enhanced human capital potentially confers a war-winning (and deterring) advantage.

Increasing and diversifying the military human capital stock will mean more training, and attention to getting more return in the form of longer terms of military service. This may well lead to major reforms in US military personnel systems (long overdue in our opinion).

Also, a need for more training will also increase demand for IT-based training systems. For every training need, there is an optimum mix of live versus simulated environments. As simulators get better and cheaper, and live training gets more expensive, simulators will inevitably assume a larger role. This will, in turn, increase the market for military training devices.

## 6.4 The Continuing Problem of Defense Resources

In the past, defense budgets have been cyclical in nature – rising and falling with assessed security threats. Even with security threats rising, a cyclical upturn in defense budgets is unlikely. First, as discussed earlier, the United States is expected to achieve slow economic growth (<2%) for the indefinite future. Second, nondefense, "mandatory" (entitlement) programs are expected to increase their share of GDP for an extended period. Finally, reforms and "efficiencies," while helpful, are unlikely to resolve the strategy-resources mismatch.

Barring a major change in national strategy (Edelman and Roughead, 2018, esp. p. 52), the strategy-forces-resources mismatch will likely be a chronic, sometimes acute, quandary for the US defense economy for some time to come.

## 6.5 Developments in Military-Industrial Affairs: The Sinews of Military Power

Those adverse developments in threats and resources are offset somewhat with innovations in military acquisition and sustainment. There is also the promise offered by new acquisition reform initiatives.

### 6.5.1 Digital Engineering

Advocates maintain that digital engineering[54] enables more precisely specified designs completed much quicker (Erwin, 2020a). Among other things, digital design enables wider application of additive manufacturing (3-D printing). This has clear implications for sustaining equipment (Shaw, 2018). However, the use of digital designs is likely to give rise to contention between the DoD and its suppliers. One major issue will be intellectual property rights (Trimble, Hudson and Bruno, 2019, p. 23).

### 6.5.2 Emerging Trends in International Cooperation

The F-35 program appears to have been a watershed event for international cooperation in defense systems. It was intended to meet the needs of all three US services, plus air combat arms of at least eleven other nations. The program has a troubled history for various reasons, including costs of various kinds, schedule, the heavy hand of the US export control regime,[55] and issues of "operational sovereignty" (as discussed in Franck, Lewis, and Udis, 2008, esp., pp. 88–90). The US–Turkey feud over S-400 missile systems is the most conspicuous operational sovereignty dispute.

---

[54] A concise description of digital engineering is "an integrated digital approach that uses authoritative sources of systems data and models as a continuum across disciplines" (Shepard and Scherb, 2020) – in effect, an automation of traditional engineering processes (Aureon Group, 2021).

[55] See James Arbuthnot's statement cited earlier (also Moore *et al.*, 2011, esp. pp. 73, 86).

While reasonable people can disagree over how much capability the F-35 brings, there are some clear facts. None of the many F-35 partners have expressed interest in that program as a model for the future.

Accordingly, international cooperation is moving toward program-specific joint ventures. Examples of more enduring cooperation modes follow.

(1) Germany and France (Airbus and Dassault) are proceeding with a common fighter aircraft with associated systems (FCAS; Siebold and Salaün, 2021). Spain (Indra) joined in late 2020 (Bronk, 2021).
(2) The UK and Japan have agreed to cooperate in developing aircraft subsystems for their next fighter aircraft programs (Perrett, 2021).
(3) India's preferred mode of cooperation will likely emphasize licensed production of existing military platforms (Raghuvanshi, 2020).

However, US firms are likely to be involved within these arrangements as suppliers, like engines from GE for a new Korean fighter (Waldron, 2019).

The United States itself appears headed toward extensive cooperation with its NTIB[56] – the United States, UK, Canada, and Australia (Peters, 2021). Current developments along these lines include the following:

(1) CAE's (Canada) recent agreement to purchase L3Harris's training systems division – which it appears will keep its current location in Florida and will enter into an SSA with the US government (Chandra, 2021a).
(2) The Loyal Wingman (unmanned escort fighter) development, which features major roles for Boeing Australia and the RAAF (Chandra, 2021b).
(3) The recent US–UK space cooperation treaty (Technology Safeguards Agreement) concluded in 2020 (Foreign, Commonwealth, and Development Office, 2021).

Key questions for these ventures include whether one nation is not enough, but two is too many. The current Franco-German controversies over intellectual property and mission capabilities of the "core air vehicle" of FCAS illustrate the difficulties that can arise in such arrangements (Bronk, 2021).

### 6.5.3 Acquisition Reform: New Paths to the Holy Grail

One of the main themes of US defense economic affairs has been a consistent belief that the defense acquisition system is in serious need of reform. This has

---

[56] One standard definition for the defense industrial base (DIB) is enterprises that provide "the products and services that enable the Department's warfighting capabilities" (Peters, 2021). The NTIB now includes Australia, Canada, the UK, and the United States. In the FY 2017 Defense Authorization Act, the NTIB was expanded to include the UK and Australia. As Peters (2021) put it "the domestic DIB and portions of the global DIB form the ... NTIB."

led to many initiatives and major legislation, but the "reformed" system that emerges is consistently found wanting.

Peter Levine[57] (2020) has recently offered an analysis of past defense management reform efforts, including "the never-ending search for acquisition reform" (pp. 82–148). He reports on the history of the reform initiatives and lessons learned. A summary of his nuanced treatment of a complex subject follows.

Past reforms proceeded in stages. First was public discontent with defense acquisition (p. 84) – typically associated with disclosure of bad results. Highly priced tools and spare parts that came to light in the early 1980s is one example.

However, actual implementation of the new directives (second stage) required sustained leadership follow-through to ensure implementation (p. 84). Thus, for example, the Carlucci initiatives (1980s) were largely abandoned before the end of the decade without implementation, "good intentions and sound policies are not enough" (p. 98).

Finally, effective reform for the long term means proper incentives (p. 84). The spare parts reforms of the 1980s were initially successful, but the pricing problems reappeared later (p. 103). The TransDigm episode is one example.

Other interesting themes emerge from Levine's analysis. First is the generally top-down approach. A "blue ribbon" commission or study group is tasked with analyzing the problems and recommending solutions. In many cases, implementation of those recommendations featured highly centralized control of the acquisition process. One example was an under secretary for acquisition directive (April 1991) that directed that significant changes to any one of the DoD's 200+ ongoing major acquisition programs should receive his approval (p. 115).

Second, acquisition reform had some successes. For example, while the Carlucci reforms went largely unimplemented, there was significant progress in cost estimation of major acquisition programs (p. 96).

Third, reforms tend not to succeed if the behavior mandated is not incentivized. Without it, reform implementation tends to be followed by "backsliding" by the agencies concerned. Moreover, successful implementation is more likely if leadership recognizes the scarcity of time and attention ("bandwidth") that can be devoted to any given issue at any given time. Therefore, prioritization of reform efforts is essential. And successful action to resolve small problems doesn't accomplish much (pp. 107, 142).

---

[57] Levine is an experienced and knowledgeable defense insider, with extensive service with the Senate Armed Services Committee and the Office of the Secretary of Defense.

### 6.5.4 New Acquisition Reform Directions

Current acquisition reform initiatives are more bottom-up than past efforts, and this trend is likely to continue. It is fair, for example, to characterize the new DoD acquisition management directive (DOD 5000.1) as intended more for "agile acquisition" than controlled process (US Department of Defense, 2020b). "Other Transactions Authorities" of various kinds are finding increasing application in DoD programs (Harper, 2019).

Given a more decentralized approach to reforms, a large number and variety of acquisition improvement efforts are now undergoing – with 63 reform initiatives noted by Levine (2020, p. 120). While the efficacy of the associated incentives is yet to be determined, the current efforts are likely to be more in keeping with organizational norms and could well be more successful than past efforts.

In short, a number of acquisition reforms efforts are underway. We expect some of them to succeed and reshape the defense economy.

### 6.5.5 Schedule

There is a perpetual tension between proceeding, with prudence versus fielding needed capabilities quickly. Current thinking in the DoD is, for a number of reasons,[58] tending more toward acquiring new capabilities expeditiously. For at least the near future, it is likely "quickly" will be weighed more heavily in program management decisions.

### 6.5.6 Improved Engineering Methods

> Our complexity reach exceeds our engineering grasp. (Well-informed DoD official, 2012)[59]

One measure that promises better speed with prudence is digital engineering. Examples include the Air Force NGAD (Next-Generation Air Dominance) system (Insinna, 2020; Rogoway, 2020). Likewise, Space Force advocates digitally engineered satellites (Erwin, 2020a).

Advocates see rapid, highly accurate design processes executed in the virtual world. In short, digital engineering seeks to extend our engineering grasp of complex designs.

---

[58] These include losing a march to rivals – which is the case for hypersonic weapons, and also starting the program too late – the GBSD program.

[59] Offered under Chatham House Rules.

### 6.5.7 Improved Acquisition Process

This newer approaches to acquisition reform range from the relatively minor to quite ambitious. An example of the former is an Air Force proposal to combine GBSD MILCON appropriations in groups of projects rather than the more traditional Congressional methods (Mehta, 2020c). A more ambitious agenda is embodied in a number of proposals from Space Force (Hitchens, 2020).

### 6.5.8 Addressing Barriers to Entry and Innovation

These themes are closely intertwined. The central idea is that small startups have innovation as a core competence (Baumol, 2010, pp. 64–66); however, they cannot get these ideas to potential defense customers because of a large set of complex and costly prerequisites for doing business with the DoD (barriers to entry). In effect, the DoD seeks to address the problem by outreach programs to potential suppliers in the commercial sector.

One example of this outreach is called AFWERX. Outreach to commercial sectors is accomplished through a means such as a venture capital fund (AFWERX, 2020) and one major AFWERX purpose is guiding potential defense suppliers through the barriers between the commercial sector and the defense marketplace (AFWERX, 2020).

These newer initiatives originate within the various defense organizations, as opposed to responding to external mandates. Therefore, they will likely be more consistent with organizational norms and be more enduring than previous reform efforts.

# References

Acquisition and Sustainment (2020) *Cybersecurity Maturity Model Certification (CMMC)*, v. 1.0. Available at: www.acq.osd.mil/cmmc/docs/CMMC_Model_Main_20200203.pdf (accessed: September 8, 2021).

Aeroweb (2020a) "Top-100 U.S. Government Contractors." Available at: http://fi-aeroweb.com/Top-100-US-Government-Contractors.html (accessed: November 5, 2020).

Aeroweb (2020b) "LGM-30 Minuteman III ICBM, Aeroweb." Available at: www.fi-aeroweb.com/Defense/Minuteman.html (accessed: December 3, 2020).

AFWERX (2020) Available at: www.afwerx.af.mil/ (accessed: June 30, 2021).

Aghion, P. (2003) "Empirical Estimates of the Relationship between Product Market Competition and Innovation," in Touffut, J.-P. (ed.) *Institutions, Innovation and Growth: Selected Economic Papers*. Cheltenham: Edward Elgar, pp. 142–169.

AIA (Aerospace Industries Association) (2018) "Facts and Figures: U.S. Aerospace and Defense." Available at: www.aia-aerospace.org/wp-content/uploads/2018/07/2018_-Annual-Report_Web.pdf (accessed: September 8, 2021).

Aitoro, J. (2016) "30 years: A norm Augustine retrospective," *DefenseNews*, October 25. Available at: www.defensenews.com/30th-anniversary/2016/10/25/30-years-a-norm-augustine-retrospective/ (accessed: November 7, 2020).

Amara, J. (2019) "Revisiting the Justification for an All-Volunteer Force," *Defense and Security Analysis*, 35(3), pp. 326–342. doi: 10.1080/14751798.2019.1640425.

Arena, M. V., Persons, B., Blickstein, I., *et al*. (2018) *Assessing Bid Protests of U.S. Department of Defense Procurements: Identifying Issues, Trends and Drivers*. Santa Monica, CA: RAND Corporation. Available at: www.rand.org/pubs/research_reports/RR2356.html (accessed: October 26, 2021).

Armstrong, T. H. (2019) *Re: GAO Bid Protest Annual Report to Congress for Fiscal Year 2019*. Washington, DC: Government Accountability Office. Available at: www.gao.gov/assets/710/702551.pdf (accessed: December 2, 2020).

Arnold, S. A., Harmon, B. A., Tyson, K. W., Fasana, K. G., and Wait, C. S., (2008) *Defense Department Profit and Contract Finance Policies and Their Effects on Contract and Contractor Performance*. Alexandria, VA: Institute for Defense Analysis. Available at: https://apps.dtic.mil/dtic/tr/fulltext/u2/a482081.pdf (accessed: November 9, 2020).

Asch, L. (2020) "Acquisition Tips and Tools, with Larry Asch, Acquisition Research Program," July 24. Available at: https://nps.edu/web/acqnresearch/previous-newsletters (accessed: December 2, 2020).

Associated Press (2006) "EADS-CASA cancels military plane deal," *The Washington Post*. Available at: www.washingtonpost.com/wp-dyn/content/article/2006/10/19/AR2006101900046.html (accessed: December 1, 2020).

Augustine, N. R. (1997) "Reshaping an industry: Lockheed Martin's survival story," *Harvard Business Review*, May–June. Available at: https://hbr.org/1997/05/reshaping-an-industry-lockheed-martins-survival-story (accessed: October 26, 2021).

Aureon Group (2021) "What Is Digital Engineering?" Available at: www.aurecongroup.com/expertise/digital-engineering-and-advisory/defining-digital-engineering (accessed: February 23, 2021).

Aviation Week (2020) "Faster Weapons Sales to U.S. Allies?," *Aviation Week*, 182(17), p. 8. Available at: https://aviationweek.com/sites/default/files/2020-08/AWST_200831.pdf (accessed: September 8, 2021).

BAE Systems (2019) *Annual Report 2019*. London: BAE Systems. Available at: https://investors.baesystems.com/~/media/Files/B/Bae-Systems-Investor-Relations-V3/PDFs/results-and-reports/results/2020/bae-ar-complete-2020-03-23-annual-report.pdf (accessed: November 6, 2020).

BAE Systems (2020) "Special Security Agreement." Available at: www.baesystems.com/en-us/our-company/about-us/bae-systems–inc-/special-security-agreement (accessed: October 26, 2021).

Baumol, W. J. (2002) *The Free-Market Innovation Machine: Analyzing the Growth Miracle of Capitalism*. Princeton, NJ: Princeton University Press.

Baumol, W. J. (2010) *The Microtheory of Innovative Entrepreneurship*. Princeton, NJ: Princeton University Press.

Baumol, W. J., Panzar, J. C., and Willig, R. D. (1988) *Contestable Markets and the Theory of Industry Structure*, revised. San Dieso, CA: Harcourt Brace Jovanovich.

Berger, Eric (2021), Blue Origin's powerful BE-4 engine is more than four years late—here's why, Ars Technica, https://arstechnica.com/science/2021/08/blue-origins-powerful-be-4-engine-is-more-than-four-years-late-heres-why/

Berger, E. (2019) "Four Rocket Companies Are Competing for Air Force Funding, and It Is War," *Ars Technica*. Available at: https://arstechnica.com/science/2019/08/four-rocket-companies-are-competing-for-air-force-funding-and-it-is-war/ (accessed: November 9, 2020).

Bialos, J. P., Fisher, C. E., and Koehl, S. L. (2009) *Fortresses & Icebergs. The Evolution of the Transatlantic Defense Market and the Implications for U.S. National Security Policy*. Washington, DC: Center for Transtlantic Relations;

Johns Hopkins University; US Department of Defense. Available at: https://apps.dtic.mil/dtic/tr/fulltext/u2/a531716.pdf (accessed: November 7, 2020).

Boeing (2018) "Boeing Completes Acquisition of Leading Aerospace Parts Distributor KLX Inc. to Enhance Growing Services Business," *Boeing.* Available at: https://boeing.mediaroom.com/2018-10-09-Boeing-Completes-Acquisition-of-Leading-Aerospace-Parts-Distributor-KLX-Inc-to-Enhance-Growing-Services-Business (accessed: November 8, 2020).

Boeing (2020) "United Launch Alliance," *Boeing.* Available at: www.boeing.com/space/united-launch-alliance/#/history (accessed: November 9, 2020).

Boese, W. (2005) "United States retires MX missile," *Arms Control Today.* Available at: www.armscontrol.org/act/2005-10/united-states-retires-mx-missile (accessed: October 22, 2021).

Borenstein, S. (2006) "Lockheed Martin wins NASA contract," *Associated Press.* Available at: www.washingtonpost.com/wp-dyn/content/article/2006/09/01/AR2006090100291_pf.html (accessed: September 8, 2021).

Bronk, J. (2021) "FCAS: Is the Franco-German-Spanish Combat Air Programme Really in Trouble?" *RUSI.* Available at: https://rusi.org/commentary/fcas-franco-german-spanish-combat-air-programme-really-trouble (accessed: September 8, 2021).

Brothers, E. (2017) "Rockwell Collins completes $8.6B acquisition of B/E Aerospace," *Aerospace Manufacturing and Design.* Available at: www.aerospacemanufacturinganddesign.com/article/rockwell-collins-completes-acquisition-be-aerospace-041917/ (accessed: November 9, 2020).

Bruno, M. (2020) "Growing concerns," *Aviation Week & Space Technology,* September 14–27, p. 12.

Burghardt, T. (2020) "Tory Bruno Outlines ULA Transition to Vulcan and National Security Launches," *NASASpaceFlight.com.* Available at: www.nasaspaceflight.com/2020/03/tory-bruno-ula-transition-vulcan-nssl-launches/ (accessed: November 9, 2020).

Carlson, S. (2017) "Boeing, Northrop Grumman receive development contracts for new ICBM," *United Press International,* August 22. Available at: www.spacedaily.com/reports/Boeing_Northrop_Grumman_receive_development_contracts_for_new_ICBM_999.html (accessed: October 22, 2021).

Carril, R. and Duggan, M. (2018) "The Impact of Industry Consolidation on Government Procurement: Evidence from Department of Defense Contracting." Working Paper 25160. Available at: www.nber.org/system/files/working_papers/w25160/w25160.pdf (accessed: December 8, 2020).

CBS News (2006) "Venezuela may sell U.S. jets to Iran," *CBS News*, May 16. Available at: www.cbsnews.com/news/venezuela-may-sell-us-jets-to-iran/ (accessed: October 22, 2021).

Cecire, M. H., and Peters, H. M. (2020a) *The Defense Production Act of 1950: History, Authorities, and Considerations for Congress.* Washington, DC: Congressional Research Service. Available at: https://crsreports.congress .gov/product/pdf/R/R43767 (accessed: September 9, 2020).

Cecire, M. H., and Peters, H. M. (2020b) *Defense Production Act (DPA): Recent Developments in Response to COVID-19.* Washington, DC: Congressional Research Service. Available at: https://crsreports.congress.gov/product/pdf/ IN/IN11470 (accessed: November 7, 2020).

Censer, M. (2019) "Northrop says it has received 'civil investigative demand' from Federal Trade Commission," *Inside Defense*, October 24. Available at: https://insidedefense.com/insider/northrop-says-it-has-received-civil-investi gative-demand-federal-trade-commission (accessed: October 22, 2021).

Chan, R. (2018) "Google drops out of $10 billion JEDI contract bid," *Business Insider*. Available at: www.businessinsider.de/international/google-drops- out-of-10-billion-jedi-contract-bid-2018-10/ (accessed: December 2, 2020).

Chandra, A. (2021a) "CAE Acquires L3Harris Technologies' Military Training Business," *GBP Aerospace & Defense*. Available at: https://gbp.com.sg/stor ies/cae-acquires-l3harris-technologies-military-training-business/ (accessed: September 8, 2021).

Chandra, A. (2021b) "Boeing Loyal Wingman Makes First Flight," *GBP Aerospace & Defense*. Available at: https://gbp.com.sg/stories/boeing- loyal-wingman-makes-first-flight/ (accessed: September 8, 2021).

Chapa, J. (2021) "Trust and Tech: AI Education in the Military," *War on the Rocks*. Available at: https://warontherocks.com/2021/03/trust-and-tech-ai- education-in-the-military/ (accessed: September 8, 2021).

Chaplain, C. L. (2016) *Evolved Expendable Launch Vehicle: DOD Is Assessing Data on Worldwide Launch Market to Inform New Acquisition Strategy.* Washington, DC: Government Accountability Office. Available at: www .gao.gov/assets/680/678646.pdf (accessed: November 9, 2020).

Clark, C. (2016) "F-35: DoD Forces Lockheed to Accept Its Price for LRIP 9," *Breaking Defense*. Available at: https://breakingdefense.com/2016/11/jpo-to- lockheed-no-more-talkie-heres-lrip-9-deal/ (accessed: November 9, 2020).

Clark, C. (2019) "FTC investigates Northrop: GBSD?" *Breaking Defense*, October 24. Available at: https://breakingdefense.com/2019/10/ftc-investi gates-northrop-gbsd/ (accessed October 22, 2021).

Cohen, R. S. (2019) "Boeing backs out of nuclear missile competition, prompting USAF choices," *Air Force Magazine*, July 25. Available at: www.airforcemag

.com/Features/Pages/2019/July%202019/Boeing-Pulls-Out-of-Ground-Based-Strategic-Deterrent-Program.aspx (accessed: October 22, 2021).

Cohen, R. S. (2020) "Northrop wins $13.3B contract to design new ICBMs," *Air Force Magazine*. Available at: www.airforcemag.com/northrop-wins-13-3b-contract-to-build-new-icbms/ (accessed: December 8, 2020).

Cole, J., and Lipin, S. (1996) "Boeing agrees to acquire two Rockwell businesses," *The Wall Street Journal*, August 2. Available at: www.wsj.com/articles/SB838902218460054000 (accessed: November 7, 2020).

Congressional Budget Office (2019) *Long-Term Implications of the 2020 Future Years Defense Program*. Washington, DC: Congressional Budget Office. Available at: www.cbo.gov/publication/55500 (accessed: November 3, 2020).

Congressional Budget Office Congres (2020) *An Update to the Budget Outlook: 2020–2030*. Washington, DC: Congressional Budget Office. Available at: www.cbo.gov/system/files/2020-09/56517-Budget-Outlook.pdf (accessed: November 3, 2020).

Congressional Budget Office (2021) *Estimated Budgetary Effects of H.R. 1319, the American Rescue Plan Act of 2021*, revised March 5. Washington, DC: Congressional Budget Office. Available at: www.cbo.gov/system/files/2021-03/Estimated_Budget_Effects_of_H.R._1319_as_Engrossed_by_the_House.pdf (accessed: September 8, 2021).

Congressional Research Service (2020) *Defense Primer:RDT&E*, updated April 29, Washington, DC: Congressional Research Service. Available at: https://apps.dtic.mil/sti/pdfs/AD1112838.pdf (accessed: October 21, 2021).

Cooper, D. E. (1998) *Defense Industry Consolidation Competitive Effects of Mergers and Acquisitions*. Washington, DC: Government Accountability Office . Available at: www.govinfo.gov/content/pkg/GAOREPORTS-T-NSIAD-98-112/pdf/GAOREPORTS-T-NSIAD-98-112.pdf (accessed: September 8, 2021).

Cordell, C. (2019) "FTC probes Northrop nuclear missile bid as Air Force dumps Boeing," *Washington Business Journal,* October 25. Available at: www.bizjournals.com/washington/news/2019/10/25/ftc-probes-northrop-nuclear-missilebid-as-air.html (accessed: October 22, 2021).

Crunchbase (2020) "Compare Profiles," *Crunchbase*. Available at: www.crunchbase.com/compare/organization/orbital-atk/ (accessed: December 7, 2020).

CSIS (2017) "Debate: Modernization of Nuclear Missiles." Available at: www.csis.org/events/debate-modernization-nuclear-missile (accessed October 22, 2021).

Dayen, D. (2019) "How Rep. Ro Khanna got a defense contractor to return $16 million," *The Intercept*. Available at: https://theintercept.com/2019/05/28/ro-khanna-transdigm-refund-pentagon/ (accessed: September 8, 2021).

Defense Daily Staff (2020) "House Armed Services Committee Unanimously Approves FY '21 NDAA," *Defense Daily*, July 2. Available at: www.defen sedaily.com/house-armed-services-committee-unanimously-approves-fy-21-ndaa (accessed: October 22, 2021).

Defense Industrial Daily (2005) "EADS & Northrop Grumman offer USAF an Airbus tanker option," *Defense Industry Daily*. Available at: www.defensein dustrydaily.com/eads-northrop-grumman-offer-usaf-an-airbus-tanker-option-01164/ (accessed: September 8, 2021).

Defense Manpower Data Center (2020) *DoD Personnel, Workforce Reports & Publications*. Available at: www.dmdc.osd.mil/appj/dwp/dwp_reports.jsp (accessed: November 3, 2020).

*DefenseNews* (2019) "Top 100." Available at: https://people.defensenews.com/top-100/ (accessed: November 9, 2020).

Deloitte (2016) US Aerospace and Defense Labor Market Study, https://www2 .deloitte.com/content/dam/Deloitte/us/Documents/manufacturing/us-ad-labor-market-study-2016.pdf, (Accessed November 5, 2021).

Deutch, J. (2001) "Consoludation of the U.S. Defense Industrial Base," *Acquisition Review Quarterly*, 8(3), pp. 137–150. Available at: www.dau .edu/library/arj/ARJ/arq2001/Deutch.pdf (accessed: December 8, 2020).

Directorate of Defense Trade Controls (2020a) "Home – DDTC Public Portal." Available at: www.pmddtc.state.gov/ddtc_public (accessed: December 1, 2020).

Directorate of Defense Trade Controls (2020b) "Who Must Register." Available at: www.pmddtc.state.gov/ddtc_public?id=ddtc_kb_article_page&sy s_id=7110b98edbb8d30044f9ff621f96192d (accessed: December 1, 2020).

Dwyer, M. (2019) "Does the Defense Department's New Approach to Industrial Base Cybersecurity Create More Problems Than It Solves?," *Center for Strategic and International Studies*. Available at: www.csis.org/analysis/does-defense-departments-new-approach-industrial-base-cybersecurity-cre ate-more-problems-it (accessed: November 6, 2020).

Eaglen, Mackenzie (2020), Tri-Service Modernization Crunch (2020), American Enterprise Institute, https://www.aei.org/wp-content/uploads/2021/03/The-2020s-Tri-Service-Modernization-Crunch-1.pdf?x91208

Eckstein, M. (2020), "Marines issue new doctrine prioritizing learning," *USNI News*. Available at: https://news.usni.org/2020/05/19/marines-issue-new-doctrine-prioritizing-learning (accessed: September 8, 2021).

Edelman, E., Roughead, G., Fox, C., *et al.* (2018) *Providing for the Common Defense: The Assessment and Recommendations of the National Defense Strategy Commission*. Washington, DC: The United States Institute of Peace. Available at: www.usip.org/sites/default/files/2019-07/providing-for-the-common-defense.pdf (accessed: September 8, 2021).

Encyclopedia Astronautica (2019) SICBM. Available at: www.astronautix
.com/s/sicbm.html (accessed: October 22, 2021).

Erwin, S. (2015) "Former SecDef Perry: Defense Industry Consolidation Has
Turned Out Badly," *National Defense*, December 2. Available at: www
.nationaldefensemagazine.org/articles/2015/12/2/former-secdef-perry-defense-
industry-consolidation-has-turned-out-badly (accessed: September 8, 2021).

Erwin, S. (2018a) "Acquisition of Orbital ATK approved, company renamed
Northrop Grumman Innovation Systems," *SpaceNews*. Available at: https://
spacenews.com/acquisition-of-orbital-atk-approved-company-renamed-north
rop-grumman-innovation-systems/ (accessed: September 8, 2021).

Erwin, S. (2018b) "Air Force awards launch vehicle development contracts to
Blue Origin, Northrop Grumman, ULA," *SpaceNews*. Available at: https://
spacenews.com/air-force-awards-launch-vehicle-development-contracts-to-
blue-origin-northrop-grumman-ula/ (accessed: September 8, 2021).

Erwin, S. (2018c) "Boeing to acquire Millennium Space Systems," *SpaceNews*.
Available at: https://spacenews.com/boeing-to-acquire-millennium-space-
systems/ (accessed: November 9, 2020).

Erwin, S. (2019) "HASC chairman: Single-contractor bid for new ICBM is
'troubling,'" *Space News*, October 24. Available at: https://spacenews.com/
hasc-chairman-single-contractor-bid-for-new-icbm-is-troubling/ (accessed:
October 22, 2021).

Erwin, S. (2020a) "Space Force developing a digital strategy for designing and
producing future satellites," *SpaceNews*. Available at: https://spacenews
.com/space-force-developing-a-digital-strategy-for-designing-and-produ
cing-future-satellites/ (accessed: September 8, 2021).

Erwin, S. (2020b) "Northrop Grumman to terminate OmegA rocket program,"
*SpaceNews*. Available at: https://spacenews.com/northrop-grumman-to-ter
minate-omega-rocket-program/ (accessed: November 9, 2020).

Erwin, S. (2021) "To defend the high frontier, Space Force wants digitally
minded troops," *SpaceNews*. Available at: https://spacenews.com/to-defend-
the-high-frontier-space-force-wants-digitally-minded-troops/ (accessed:
September 8, 2021).

Esterline Technologies Corporation (2018) "TransDigm to acquire Esterline
Technologies in $4 billion all cash transaction," *Global New Wire*. Available
at: www.globenewswire.com/news-release/2018/10/10/1619251/0/en/
TransDigm-to-Acquire-Esterline-Technologies-in-4-Billion-All-Cash-
Transaction.html (accessed: November 9, 2020).

Eversden, A. (2019) "JEDI: How we got here," *Federal Times*. Available at:
www.federaltimes.com/home/2019/07/10/jedi-how-we-got-here/ (accessed:
September 8, 2021).

Everstine, B. W. (2021) "Swiss Air Force knives," *Air Force Magazine*, April 2021, p. 48. Available at: www.airforcemag.com/article/swiss-air-force-knives/ (accessed: September 8, 2021).

Federal Acquisition Regulation (2020a) "Access the Federal Acquisition Regulation." Available at: www.acquisition.gov/sites/default/files/current/far/pdf/FAR.pdf (accessed: October 26, 2021).

Federal Acquisition Regulation (2020b) "15.404–4 Profit." Available at: www.acquisition.gov/far/15.404-4 (accessed: December 3, 2020).

Federal Trade Commission (2018a) "FTC Approves Modified Final Order Imposing Conditions on Northrop Grumman's Acquisition of Solid Rocket Motor Supplier Orbital ATK, Inc." Available at: www.ftc.gov/news-events/press-releases/2018/12/ftc-approves-modified-final-order-imposing-condi tions-northrop (accessed: November 9, 2020).

Federal Trade Commission (2018b) "In the Matter of Northrop Grumman Corporation: Modified Decision and Order." Available at: www.ftc.gov/system/files/documents/cases/181_0005_c-4652_northrop_grumman_orbital_atk_modi fied_decision_and_order_12-4-18.pdf (accessed: December 7, 2020).

Federation of American Scientists (2019) Ground Based Strategic Deterrent, https://www.globalsecurity.org/wmd/systems/gbsd.htm. accessed 29 November 2019.

Feickert, A. (2021) *New U.S. Marine Corps Force Design Initiatives*, IN11281. Washington, DC: Congressional Research Service.

Fergusson, I. F., and Kerr, P. K. (2020) *The U.S. Export Control System and the Export Control Reform Initiative*. Washington, DC: Congressional Research Service. Available at: https://fas.org/sgp/crs/natsec/R41916.pdf (accessed: December 1, 2020).

Field, L. A. (2017) *"Myth-Busting 3" Further Improving Industry Communication with Effective Debriefings*. Washington, DC: The White House. Available at: https://obamawhitehouse.archives.gov/sites/default/files/omb/procurement/memo/myth-busting_3_further_improving_industry_communications_with_effectiv....pdf (accessed: October 26, 2021).

Flfrick, A. (2005) *Rivet MILE Reaches Milestone, MissileNews.com*. Available at: www.missilenews.com/space-command-news/rivet-mile-reaches-milest.shtml (accessed: December 3, 2020).

Foreign, Commonwealth, and Development Office (2021) "UK–US Technology Safeguards Agreement (TSA) for Spaceflight Activities: Understanding the TSA," February 8 (update). Available at: www.gov.uk/government/publications/ukusa-agreement-in-the-form-of-an-exchange-of-notes-between-the-united-kingdom-and-the-united-states-of-america-on-technology-safeguards-associated/uk-us-technology-safe guards-agreement-tsa-for-spaceflight-activities-understanding-the-tsa (accessed: September 8, 2021).

Fox, J. R., Allen, D. G., Lassman, T. C., Moody, W. S., and Shiman, P. L. (2011) *Defense Acquisition Reform 1960–2009: An Elusive Goal*. Washington, DC: Center for Military History. Available at: https://history.army.mil/html/ books/051/51-3-1/CMH_Pub_51-3-1.pdf (accessed: December 8, 2020).

Franck, R., Hildebrandt, G., and Udis, B. (2016) "Toward Realistic Acquisition Schedule Estimates," in *Proceedings of the Thirteenth Annual Acquisition Research Symposium*. Monterey, CA: Naval Postgraduate School. Available at: https://nps.edu/documents/105938399/108639550/SYM-AM-16-029.pdf/ 12c9563c-164f-495d-935f-8b4b969d31d2 (accessed: November 9, 2020).

Franck, R., Lewis, I., and Udis, B. (2008) *Echoes across the Pond: Understanding EU-US Defense Industrial Relationships*. Monterey, CA: Naval Postgraduate School, NPS-AM-08–002 (revised May 20).

Franck, R. E., Lewis, I., and Udis, B. (2012) *Global Aerospace Industries: Rapid Changes Ahead?* Monterey, CA: Naval Postgraduate School. Available at: http:// hdl.handle.net/10945/33846 (accessed: December 2, 2020).

Franck, R., and Udis, B. (2017) "Quarrelsome Committees in US Defense Acquisition: the KC-X Case," *Defence and Peace Economics*, 28(3), pp. 344–366. doi: 10.1080/10242694.2015.1073488.

Freed, J. (2011) "Boeing CEO: 'New airplane' to replace 737," *NBC News*. Available at: www.nbcnews.com/id/wbna41517601 (accessed: December 8, 2020).

Freedberg Jr., S. J. (2019) "Amazon's big JEDI gamble ANALYSIS," *Breaking Defense*. Available at: https://breakingdefense.com/2019/11/amazons-big- jedi-gamble-analysis/ (accessed: December 2, 2020).

Freedberg Jr., S. J. (2020) "No winner likely in JEDI court battle; 'Just Pull The Plug?': Greenwalt," *Breaking Defense*. Available at: https://breakingdefense .com/2020/04/no-winner-likely-in-jedi-court-battle-just-pull-the-plug-green walt/ (accessed: December 2, 2020).

Freeman, M., and Lyons, T. (2020) "Education Is the Technology the Navy Needs Most," in *US Naval Institute Proceedings* (July). Annapolis, MD: US Naval Institute. Available at: www.usni.org/magazines/proceedings/2020/ july/education-technology-navy-needs-most (accessed: September 8, 2021).

FundingUniverse (2020) "General Dynamics Corporation History." Available at: www.fundinguniverse.com/company-histories/general-dynamics-corpor ation-history/ (accessed: September 8, 2021).

Future of Defense Task Force Report 2020, HASC, Accessed at https://www .theblackvault.com/documentarchive/future-of-defense-task-force-report-2020/

Gallacher, D. (2019) "'Buy American' (Again): New Executive Order Requires Changes (By 2020)," *Government Contracts & Investigations Blog.* Available at: www.governmentcontractslawblog.com/2019/07/articles/baa-and-taa/baa-buy-american-again/ (accessed: September 8, 2021).

Gartzke, U. (2010) *The Boeing/McDonnell Douglas and EADS Mergers: Ethnocentric vs. Regiocentric Consolidation in the Aerospace and Defence Industry and the Implications for International Relation.* London: London School of Economics and Political Science. Available at: https://etheses.lse.ac.uk/266/1/Gartzke_Boeing%20-%20McDonnell%20Douglas%20and%20EADS%20Mergers.pdf (accessed: September 9, 2021).

Gates, D. (2006) "Separation anxiety – The wall between military and commercial technology," *Seattle Times*, January 22.

Gates, R. M. (2014) *Duty: Memoirs of a Secretary at War.* New York: Knopf.

General Dynamics (2020) Available at: www.gd.com/ (accessed: November 7, 2020).

Global Security (2020a) "Ground Based Strategic Deterrent (GBSD)." Available at: www.globalsecurity.org/wmd/systems/gbsd.htm (accessed: December 3, 2020).

Global Security (2020b) "LGM-30 Minuteman III ICBM Modernization." Available at: www.globalsecurity.org/wmd/systems/lgm-30_3-mod.htm (accessed: December 3, 2020).

Gould, J. (2019) "House armed services chairman takes aim at Air Force's handling of ICBM replacement program," *Defense News*, October 24. Available at: www.defensenews.com/congress/2019/10/24/hasc-chair-takes-aim-at-air-forces-handling-of-icbm-replacement-program/ (accessed: October 22, 2021).

Greenfield, V. A., and Brady, R. R. (2008) "The Changing Shape of the Defense Industry and Implications for Defense Acquisitions and Policy," in *Excerpt from the Proceedings of the Fifth Annual Acquisition Research Symposium.* Monterey, CA: Naval Postgraduate School. Available at: https://apps.dtic.mil/dtic/tr/fulltext/u2/a493916.pdf (accessed: November 9, 2020).

Gregg, A. (2019) "Boeing, Northrop Spar over $85 Billion Nuclear Missile Program," *Washington Post*, September 21. Available at: www.washingtonpost.com/business/2019/09/21/boeing-northrop-spar-over-billion-nuclear-missile-program/ (accessed: October 22, 2021).

Gunzinger, Mark, Carl Rehberg and Gillian Evans (2018), Sustaining the U.S. Nuclear Deterrent: The LRSO and GBSD, Center for Strategic and Budgetary Assessments, https://csbaonline.org/uploads/documents/CSBA6318-GBSD_LRSO_Report_web.pdf

Hallman, W. (2019) "Another CR, another blow to national security," *National Defense*, December 3. Available at: www.nationaldefensemagazine.org/art

icles/2019/12/3/ndia-perspective-another-cr-another-blow-to-national-secur ity (accessed: October 21, 2021).

Harper, J. (2019) "OTA agreements exploding in popularity," *National Defense*, July 9. Available at: www.nationaldefensemagazine.org/articles/2019/7/9/ ota-agreements-exploding-in-popularity (accessed: September 8, 2021).

Harper, Jon (2020) Air Force Hopes to Jettison Pass-Through Budget, National Defense Magazine, https://www.nationaldefensemagazine.org/articles/2020/ 10/29/air-force-hopes-to-jettison-pass-through-budget

Harrison, T., and Linck, E. (2017) *Options for the Ground-Based Leg of the Nuclear Triad.* Washington, DC: Center for Strategic and International Studies. Available at: https://csis-website-prod.s3.amazonaws.com/s3fs-pub lic/publication/170925_Harrison_OptionsGroundBasedLegNuclear Triad_pages.pdf (accessed: December 3, 2020).

Hartley, K. (2017) *The Economics of Arms.* New York: Agenda Publishing.

Hartmann, L., Cissell, J., and Rendon, R. (2020) *Noncompetitive Contracting: Lessons from Contracting Personnel.* Monterey, CA: Naval Postgraduate School. Available at: https://dair.nps.edu/bitstream/123456789/4214/1/ SYM-AM-20-065.pdf (accessed: October 22, 2021).

Heidenkamp, H., Louth, J., and Taylor, T. (2013) "Strategic Options," *RUSI*, 158(2), pp. 86–92. doi: 10.1080/03071847.2013.774642.

Hensel, N. (2010) "Can Industry Consolidation Lead to Greater Efficiencies? Evidence From the U.S. Defense Industry," *Business Economics*, 45(3), pp. 187–203. doi: 10.1057/be.2010.15.

Hicks, J. R. (1935) "The Best of All Monopoly Profits Is a Quiet Life," *Innovative Trust.* Available at: https://innovativetrust.wordpress.com/2011/04/19/the-best- of-all-monopoly-profits-is-a-quiet-life/ (accessed: November 9, 2020).

Hitch, C. J., McKean, R. N., and Enke, S., (1960) *The Economics of Defense in the Nuclear Age.* Boston: Harvard University Press. Available at: https:// books.google.com.ag/books?id=PYgvAAAAYAAJ&source=gbs _navlinks_s (accessed: November 30, 2020).

Hitchens, T. (2020) "Space chief targets red tape to speed new tech," *Breaking Defense.* Available at: https://breakingdefense.com/2020/09/space-chief-tar gets-red-tape-to-speed-new-tech/ (accessed: September 8, 2021).

Hoff, R. V. (2007) *Analysis of Defense Industry Consolidation Effects on Program Aquisition Costs.* Monterey, CA: Naval Postgraduate School. Available at: https://apps.dtic.mil/dtic/tr/fulltext/u2/a475971.pdf (accessed: November 7, 2020).

House Armed Services Committee (2020) *William M. (Mac)Thornberry National Defense Authorization Act for Fiscal Year 2021*, December.

Available at: https://docs.house.gov/billsthisweek/20201207/CRPT-116hrpt617.pdf (accessed: October 22, 2021).

Hoyle, C. (2006) "Flight Interview: Ronald Sugar, CEO Northrop Grumman," *Fight Global*. Available at: www.flightglobal.com/flight-interview-ronald-sugar-ceo-northrop-grumman/65509.article (accessed: November 9, 2020).

Insinna, V. (2020) "The US Air Force has built and flown a mysterious full-scale prototype of its future fighter jet," *Air Force Times*. Available at: www.airforcetimes.com/breaking-news/2020/09/15/the-us-air-force-has-built-and-flown-a-mysterious-full-scale-prototype-of-the-future-fighter-jet/ (accessed: September 8, 2021).

Insinna, V., and Losey, S. (2020) "US Air Force bails on Mattis-era fighter jet readiness goal," *DefenseNews*, May 7. Available at: www.defensenews.com/air/2020/05/07/the-air-force-bails-on-mattis-era-fighter-jet-readiness-goal/ (accessed: September 8, 2021).

Jackson, J. K. (2020) *The Committee on Foreign Investment in the United States (CFIUS)*. Washington, DC: Congressional Research Service. Available at: https://crsreports.congress.gov (accessed: November 6, 2020).

Jacobs, K. (2011) "UPDATE 2-Northrop ship spin-off expects flat sales," *Reuters*, March 31. Available at: www.reuters.com/article/northrop/update-2-northrop-ship-spin-off-expects-flat-sales-idUSN3110702820110331 (accessed: November 9, 2020).

Johnson, D. B. (2019) "Weak links in the defense supply chain," *FCW*, March 31. Available at: https://fcw.com/articles/2019/03/31/defense-sup ply-chain-weak-links.aspx (accessed: November 6, 2020).

Kalia, S. (2018) "Boeing to buy aerospace parts maker KLX for about $3.2 billion," *Reuters*, May 1. Available at: www.reuters.com/article/us-klx-m-a-boeing-idUSKBN1I22SZ (accessed: November 9, 2020).

Kerr, P. K. (2020) *Arms Sales: Congressional Review Process*. Washington, DC: Congressional Research Service. Available at: https://crsreports.con gress.gov (accessed: December 1, 2020).

Kilcullen, D. (2020) *The Dragons and the Snakes: How the Rest Learned to Fight the West*. Oxford: Oxford University Press. doi: 10.1093/oso/9780190265687.001.0001.

Kosiak, S. (2019) "Small Satellites in the Emerging Space Environment," *Center for a New American Security*, October 25. Available at: www.cnas.org/publications/reports/small-satellites-in-the-emerging-space-environ ment (accessed: November 9, 2020).

Kovacic, W. E., and Smallwood, D. E. (1994) "Competition Policy, Rivalries, and Defense Industry Consolidation," *Journal of Economic Perspectives*, 8 (4), pp. 91–110. doi: 10.1257/jep.8.4.91.

Levine, P. (2020) *Defense Management Reform*. Stanford, CA: Stanford University Press.

Magnuson, S. (2018) "The Magic of Other Transaction Authorities," *National Defense*, March 30. Available at: www.nationaldefensemagazine.org/articles/2018/3/30/the-magic-of-other-transaction-authorities (accessed: September 8, 2021).

Masters, J., and McBride, J. (2018) "Foreign Investment and U.S. National Security," *Council on Foreign Relations*. Available at: www.cfr.org/backgrounder/foreign-investment-and-us-national-security (accessed: September 8, 2021).

Mattioli, D., Cimilluca, D., and Cameron, D. (2018) "Harris, L3 Technologies announce merger plan," *The Wall Street Journal*, October 14. Available at: www.wsj.com/articles/military-communications-firms-harris-l3-near-deal-to-combine-1539443888 (accessed: September 8, 2021).

McBride, C. (2019) "Trump administration prepares sale of F-16s to Taiwan," *The Wall Street Journal*, August 16. Available at: www.wsj.com/articles/trump-administration-prepares-sale-of-f-16s-to-taiwan-11565983860 (accessed: September 8, 2021).

McGarry, B. W. (2020) *Defense Primer: Planning, Programming, Budgeting and Execution (PPBE) Process*. Washington, DC: Congressional Research Service. Available at: https://fas.org/sgp/crs/natsec/IF10429.pdf (accessed: September 8, 2021).

McGarry, B. W., and Peters, H. M. (2020) *Defense Primer: Future Years Defense Program (FYDP)*. Washington, DC: Congressional Research Service. Available at: https://crsreports.congress.gov (accessed: November 2, 2020).

McKinnon, J. D., and Tilley, A. (2019) "Pentagon picks Microsoft for JEDI Cloud-computing contract over Amazon," *The Wall Street Journal*, October 25. Available at: www.wsj.com/articles/pentagon-picksmicrosoft-for-jedi-cloud-computing-contract-over-amazon-11572045221 (accessed: September 8, 2021).

Mehta, A. (2018a) "General Dynamics completes CSRA acquisition," *DefenseNews*, April 3. Available at: www.defensenews.com/industry/2018/04/03/general-dynamics-completes-csra-acquisition/ (accessed: November 9, 2020).

Mehta, A. (2018b) "State Department cleared $70 billion in foreign military sales requests for FY18," *DefenseNews*, October 5. Available at: www.defensenews.com/global/2018/10/05/state-department-cleared-70-billion-in-foreign-military-sales-requests-for-fy18/ (accessed: December 1, 2020).

Mehta, A. (2019) "SAIC completes $2.5B engility acquisition deal," *DefenseNews*, January 15. Available at: www.defensenews.com/industry/2019/01/15/saic-com pletes-25b-engility-acquisition-deal/ (accessed: November 9, 2020).

Mehta, A. (2020a) "To keep weapon sales in place, US offers new options for payment," *DefenseNews*, August 4. Available at: www.defensenews.com/ pentagon/2020/08/04/to-keep-weapon-sales-in-place-us-offers-new-options-for-payment/ (accessed: December 1, 2020).

Mehta, A. (2020b) "US weapon sales boss talks China, arms exports and his agency's future," *DefenseNews*, August 3. Available at: www.defensenews .com/interviews/2020/08/03/us-weapon-sales-boss-talks-china-arms-exports-and-his-agencys-future/ (accessed: December 1, 2020).

Mehta, A. (2020c) "DoD seeks legislative help for ICBM replacement con struction costs," *DefenseNews*, September 25. Available at: www.defense news.com/smr/nuclear-arsenal/2020/09/25/dod-seeking-legislative-help-for-icbm-replacement-construction-costs/ (accessed: September 8, 2021).

Melese, F. (2018) *Cost-Benefit Analysis of Bid Protests: A Representative Bidder Model*. Monterey, CA: Naval Postgraduate School. Available at: http://hdl.handle.net/10945/58754 (accessed: December 2, 2020).

Merle, R. (2001) "Northrop seals deal to buy Newport News," *The Washington Post*, September 11. Available at: www.washingtonpost.com/archive/busi ness/2001/11/09/northrop-seals-deal-to-buy-newport-news/b3f7827a-7169-4f57-823d-e8834c9b1385/ (accessed: November 9, 2020).

Mintz, J. (1997) "How a dinner led to a feeding frenzy," *The Washington Post*, July 4. Available at: www.washingtonpost.com/archive/business/1997/07/ 04/how-a-dinner-led-to-a-feeding-frenzy/13961ba2-5908–4992–8335-c3c087cdebc6/ (accessed: September 8, 2021).

Minuteman Missile (2011) "Minuteman Missile – The Beginning." Available at: https://minutemanmissile.com/ (accessed: December 3, 2020).

Mizokami, K. (2021) "The Marine Corps is about to reinvent itself – Drastically," *Popular Mechanics*, April 2. Available at: www.popularmecha nics.com/military/weapons/a36005513/us-marine-corps-historic-reinven tion/ (accessed: October 21, 2021).

Moore, D., Ito, P., Young, S., *et al.* (2011) "The Impact of U.S. Export Control and Technology Transfer Regime on the Joint Strike Fighter (JSF) Project – A UK Perspective," *Proceedings of the Eighth Annual Acquisition Research Symposium*, vol. I, pp. 72–90, NPS-AM-11-C8P03R01-025. Monterey, CA: Naval Postgraduate School. Available at: https://apps.dtic.mil/dtic/tr/fulltext/ u2/a543870.pdf (accessed: September 8, 2021).

Murphy, K. J., and Dial, J. (1993) *General Dynamics: Compensation and Strategy (A)*. Cambirdge, MA: Harvard Business School. Available at:

https://store.hbr.org/product/general-dynamics-compensation-and-strategy-a/494048 (accessed: November 7, 2020).

National Security Commission on Artificial Intelligence (2021) *Draft Final Report.* Available at: www.nscai.gov/wp-content/uploads/2021/01/NSCAI-Draft-Final-Report-1.19.21.pdf (accessed: September 8, 2021).

Neal, M. (2020) "Vulcan on Track as ULA Eyes Early-2021 Test Flight to the Moon," *NASASpaceFlight.com.* Available at: www.nasaspaceflight.com/2020/06/vulcan-2021-moon-flight/ (accessed: November 9, 2020).

Nickelsburg, M. (2019) "What is JEDI? Explaining the $10B Military cloud contract that Microsoft just won over Amazon," *GeekWire*, October 28. Available at: www.geekwire.com/2019/jedi-explaining-10b-military-cloud-con tract-microsoft-just-won-amazon/ (accessed: December 2, 2020).

Northrop–Grumman and Orbital–ATK (2017) "Northrop Grumman to Acquire Orbital ATK for $9.2 Billion," July 18. Available at: https://web.archive.org/web/20180127143225/https:/www.orbitalatk.com/news-room/publications/files/NG_PR.pdf (accessed: September 8, 2021).

Office of the Director of National Intelligence (2020) "NCSC Unveils New Supply Chain Risk Management Guidance." Available at: www.dni.gov/index.php/ncsc-newsroom/item/2153-ncsc-unveils-new-supply-chain-risk-management-guidance (accessed: November 6, 2020).

Office of the General Counsel Department of Defense (2017) *DoD Directive 5000.62 Review of Mergers, Acquisitions, Joint Venture, Investment, and Strategic Alliances of Major Defense Suppliers on National Security and Public Interest.* Washington, DC: Department of Defense. Available at: www.esd.whs.mil/Portals/54/Documents/DD/issuances/dodd/500062p.pdf (accessed: December 8, 2020).

Office of the Under Secretary of Defense (2020a) *National Defense Budget Estimates for FY 2021* (Green Book). Washington, DC: Office of the Under Secretary of Defense. Available at: https://comptroller.defense.gov/Portals/45/Documents/defbudget/fy2021/FY21_Green_Book.pdf (accessed: September 8, 2021).

Office of the Under Secretary of Defense (2020b) *Defense Budget Overview. Irreversible Implementation of the National Defense Strategy.* Washington, DC: Office of the Under Secretary of Defense. Available at: www.hsdl.org/?view&did=834722(accessed: October 26, 2021).

O'Hanlon, M. (2018) "Forecasting Change in Military Technology, 2020–2040," *Brookings*, September. Available at: www.brookings.edu/research/forecasting-change-in-military-technology-2020-2040/ (accessed: October 26, 2021).

O'Hanlon, M., Snyder, M., and Brown, A. (2020) "The Defense Industrial Base and the Future of Warfare," *Brookings*, October 23. Available at: www

.brookings.edu/events/the-defense-industrial-base-and-the-future-of-war
fare/, video at https://youtu.be/6a74NkuAOsQ (accessed: October 22, 2021).

O'Rourke, R. (2021) *Defense Primer: Naval Forces Congressional Research
Service* (updated February 10), IF104886. Washington, DC: Congressional
Research Service. Available at: https://crsreports.congress.gov/product/pdf/
IF/IF10486/22 (accessed: October 26, 2021).

Page, J. (2010) "China clones, sells Russian fighter jets," *The Wall Street Journal*,
December 4. Available at: www.wsj.com/articles/SB100014240527
4870467920457564647265569884 (accessed: September 8, 2021).

Peck, M. (2016) "Four Companies Dominate the Military Drone Market,"
*C4ISRNet*. Available at: www.c4isrnet.com/unmanned/uas/2016/04/06/four-com
panies-dominate-the-military-drone-market/ (accessed: December 8, 2020).

Perrett, B. (2021) "Japanese–UK Cooperation: Shaping New Combat Air
Systems?" *ASPI Strategist*. Available at: www.aspistrategist.org.au/japan-
and-uk-move-towards-partnership-to-develop-combat-aircraft-systems/
(accessed: September 8, 2021).

Peters, H. M. (2019a) *The Department of Defense's JEDI Cloud Program.*
Washington, DC: Congressional Research Service. Available at: https://fas
.org/sgp/crs/natsec/R45847.pdf (accessed: December 2, 2020).

Peters, H. M. (2019b) *Amazon Protest of the Department of Defense's JEDI
Cloud Contract Award to Microsoft.* Washington, DC: Congressional
Research Service. Available at: https://crsreports.congress.gov/product/pdf/
IN/IN11203 (accessed: December 2, 2020).

Peters, H. M. (2021) *Defense Primer: The National Technology and Industrial
Base*, IF11311. Washington, DC: Congressional Research Service. Available
at: https://crsreports.congress.gov/product/pdf/IF/IF11311 (accessed: October
26, 2021).

Petersen, M. (2014) "Congress oks bill banning purchases of Russian-made
rocket engines," *Los Angeles Times*, December 12. Available at: www
.latimes.com/business/la-fi-russian-rocket-ban-20141213-story.html
(accessed: November 9, 2020).

Pickar, C., and Franck, R. E. (2021) "It's About Time: Toward Realistic
Acquisition Schedule Estimates, Naval Postgraduate School," *Proceedings
of the Eighth Annual Acquisition Research Symposium*, vol. III. Monterey,
CA: Naval Postgraduate School. Available at: https://dair.nps.edcu/handle/
123456789/4323 (accessed: September 8, 2021).

Platzer, M. (2020) *Buying American: The Berry and Kissell Amendments.*
Washington, DC: Congressional Research Service. Available at: https://crsre
ports.congress.gov/product/pdf/IF/IF10605 (accessed: November 5, 2020).

PR Newswire (2019) "TransDigm Completes Acquisition of Esterline Technologies," *PR Newswire*. Available at: www.prnewswire.com/news-releases/transdigm-completes-acquisition-of-esterline-technologies-300812443.html (accessed: November 9, 2020).

Raghuvanshi, V. (2020) "Indian Air Force restructures $17 billion fighter jet program," *DefenseNews*, May 21. Available at: www.defensenews.com/global/asia-pacific/2020/05/21/indian-air-force-restructures-17-billion-fighter-jet-program/ (accessed: September 8, 2021).

Reference for Business (2020) "Rockwell International Corporation – Company Profile, Information, Business Description, History, Background Information on Rockwell International Corporation," *Reference for Business*. Available at: www.referenceforbusiness.com/history2/71/Rockwell-International-Corporation.html (accessed: November 7, 2020).

Rehberg, C. (2019) "GBSD: An imperative without delay," *Real Clear Defense*, November 21. Available at: www.realcleardefense.com/articles/2019/11/21/gbsd_an_imperative_without_delay_114860.html (accessed October 22, 2021).

Reif, K. (2021) "Biden administration begins nuclear posture review," *Arms Control Today*, September. Available at: www.armscontrol.org/act/2021-09/news/biden-administration-begins-nuclear-posture-review (accessed: October 22, 2021).

Reig, R. W. (2000) "Baseline Acquisition Reform," *Acquisition Review Quarterly*, 7(1), pp. 33–46. Available at: https://apps.dtic.mil/dtic/tr/fulltext/u2/a487528.pdf (accessed: December 8, 2020).

Reuters (2018a) "France says it must use fewer U.S. parts in its weapons systems," *Reuters*, September 6. Available at: www.reuters.com/article/us-france-defence/france-says-it-must-use-fewer-u-s-parts-in-its-weapons-systems-idUSKCN1LM2CK (accessed: December 1, 2020).

Reuters (2018b) "U.S. approves United Tech purchase of Rockwell Collins," *Reuters*, October 1. Available at: www.reuters.com/article/us-utc-m-a-rockwell-collins/us-approves-united-tech-purchase-of-rockwell-collins-idUSKCN1MB3V1 (accessed: November 9, 2020).

Ricks, T. E., and Cole, J. (1998) "How Lockheed and Northrop had their merger shot down," *The Wall Street Journal*, June 19. Available at: www.wsj.com/articles/SB898139629613188500 (accessed: November 7, 2020).

Rogerson, W. (1992) *Profit Regulation of Defense Contractors and Prizes for Innovation*. Santa Monica, CA: RAND Corporation. Available at: www.rand.org/pubs/reports/R3635.html (accessed: November 9, 2020).

Rogoway, T. (2020) "The Air Force's Secret Next Gen Air Dominance Demonstrator Isn't What You Think It Is," *The Drive*. Available at: www

.thedrive.com/the-war-zone/36509/the-air-forces-secret-next-gen-air-domin ance-demonstrator-isnt-what-you-think-it-is (accessed: September 8, 2021).

Ross, R., Pillitteri, V., Dempsey, K., Riddle, M., and Guissanie, G. (2020) "Protecting Controlled Unclassified Information in Nonfederal Systems and Organizations," NIST Special Publication 800-171. Washington, DC. doi: 10.6028/NIST.SP.800-171r2.

Sargent, J. F., Jr. (2020). *Department of Defense Research, Development, Test, and Evaluation (RDT&E): Appropriations Structure*. Washington, DC: Congressional Research Service. Updated October 7. Available at : https://crsre ports.congress.gov/product/pdf/R/R44711/9 (accessed October 16, 2021).

Schaefer, S. (2020) "Assessing the State of the Air Force: A Conversation with General David Goldfein," *Brookings*. Available at: www.brookings.edu/ events/assessing-the-state-of-the-air-force-a-conversation-with-general-david-goldfein/ (accessed: December 8, 2020).

Schneider, G. (2001) "Northrop completes purchase of Litton," *The Washington Post*, April 4. Available at: www.washingtonpost.com/archive/business/ 2001/04/04/northrop-completes-purchase-of-litton/f8e5729e-23ce-4787-bc53-90f4bd301a68/ (accessed: November 9, 2020).

Schwartz, M., and Manuel, K. M. (2015) *GAO Bid Protests: Trends and Analysis Specialist in Defense Acquisition*. Washington, DC: Congressional Research Service. Available at: https://fas.org/sgp/crs/misc/R40227.pdf (accessed: December 2, 2020).

Selyukh, A. (2019) "Pentagon Pauses $10 Billion Contract That Embroiled Amazon in Controversy," *National Public Radio*. Available at: www.npr.org/ 2019/08/01/747374991/pentagon-pauses-10-billion-cloud-contract-after-months-of-controversy (accessed: December 2, 2020).

Sensagent (2020) "Jarndyce and Jarndyce," *Sensagent*. Available at: http://dic tionary.sensagent.com/Jarndyce and Jarndyce/en-en/ (accessed: December 2, 2020).

Serbu, J. (2016), "Air Force creates new office to crunch human capital data," *Federal News Radio*. Available at: http://federalnewsradio.com/on-dod/ 2016/10/air-force-creates-new-office-crunch-human-capital-data/ (accessed: September 8, 2021).

Serbu, J. (2020) "AWS files yet another JEDI protest, challenges DoD's process for reconsidering the contract," *Federal News Network*. Available at: https:// federalnewsnetwork.com/defense-main/2020/05/aws-files-yet-another-jedi-protest-challenging-dods-process-for-reconsidering-the-contract/ (accessed: December 2, 2020).

Shackleton, R. (2020) *An Update to the Economic Outlook: 2020 to 2030*. Washington, DC: Congressional Budget Office. Available at: www.cbo

.gov/system/files/2020–07/56442-CBO-update-economic-outlook.pdf (accessed: November 3, 2020).

Shaw, M. (2018) "3D Printing in Support of the F-35," *SLDInfo.com*, July 29. Available at: https://sldinfo.com/2018/07/3d-printing-in-support-of-the-f-35/ (accessed: October 26, 2021).

Shelsby, T. (1995) "How the deal was done: The Lockheed Martin Marietta merger," *Baltimore Sun*, March 12. Available at: www.baltimoresun.com/news/bs-xpm-1995–03–12–1995071023-story.html (accessed: December 8, 2020).

Shepard, D., and Scherb, J. (2020) "What Is Digital Engineering and How Is It Related to DevSecOps?" *Carnegie Mellon University*. Available at: https://insights.sei.cmu.edu/sei_blog/2020/11/what-is-digital-engineering-and-how-is-it-related-to-devsecops.html (accessed: September 8, 2021).

Shepardson, D. (2020) "U.S. judge says Amazon likely to succeed on key argument in contract challenge," *Reuters*, March 7. Available at: https://uk.reuters.com/article/us-amazon-com-pentagon-idUKKBN20U0QC (accessed: December 2, 2020).

Siebold, S., and Salaün, T. (2021) "Berlin and Paris in crisis talks to bring fighter jet project back on track," *Reuters*, February 17. Available at: www.reuters.com/article/us-germany-france-defence-idUSKBN2AH2I8 (accessed: September 8, 2021).

Sindreu, J. (2020) "Defense deal will pose an early test for Biden administration," *The Wall Street Journal*, December 23. Available at: www.wsj.com/articles/defense-deal-will-pose-an-early-test-for-biden-administration-11608728174 (accessed: September 8, 2021).

SIPRI (2019) "Global Arms Trade: USA Increases Dominance; Arms Flows to the Middle East Surge, Says SIPRI," *SIPRI*. Available at: www.sipri.org/media/press-release/2019/global-arms-trade-usa-increases-dominance-arms-flows-middle-east-surge-says-sipri (accessed: December 1, 2020).

SIPRI (2020a) "SIPRI Military Expenditure Database," *SIPRI*. Available at: www.sipri.org/databases/milex (accessed: March 20, 2020).

SIPRI (2020b) "SIPRI Arms Transfers Database," *SIPRI*. Available at: www.sipri.org/databases/armstransfers (accessed: November 30, 2020).

SIPRI (2020c) "SIPRI Arms Transfers Database – Methodology," *SIPRI*. Available at: www.sipri.org/databases/armstransfers/background (accessed: November 30, 2020).

Solow, R. (2003) "Introduction," in Touffut, J.-P. (ed.) *Institutions, Innovation and Growth: Selected Economic Papers*. Cheltenham: Edward Elgar, pp. 1–3. Available at: https://books.google.com/books/about/Institutions_Innovation_and_Growth.html?id=jzDIngEACAAJ (accessed: December 8, 2020).

Stone, M. (2020) "U.S. Army vehicle competition halts after lone entry falls short: Official," *Reuters*, January 16. Available at: www.reuters.com/article/us-usa-pentagon-bradley/u-s-army-vehicle-competition-halts-after-lone-entry-falls-short-official-idUSKBN1ZF2RT (accessed: December 8, 2020).

The White House (2010) *Fact Sheet on the President's Export Control Reform Initiative*. Washington, DC: The White House. Available at: https://obama whitehouse.archives.gov/the-press-office/fact-sheet-presidents-export-con trol-reform-initiative (accessed: December 1, 2020).

The White House (2013) *Executive Order 13637-Administration of Reformed Export Controls*. Washington, DC: The White House. Available at: www .govinfo.gov/content/pkg/DCPD-201300143/pdf/DCPD-201300143.pdf (accessed: December 1, 2020).

The White House (2017) *National Security Strategy of the United States of America*. Washington, DC: The White House. Available at: www.white house.gov/wp-content/uploads/2017/12/NSS-Final-12–18–2017–0905.pdf (accessed: November 3, 2020).

The White House (2018a) *Presidential Order Regarding the Proposed Takeover of Qualcomm Incorporated by Broadcom Limited*. Washington, DC: The White House. Available at: www.whitehouse.gov/presidential-actions/presi dential-order-regarding-proposed-takeover-qualcomm-incorporated-broad com-limited/ (accessed: November 6, 2020).

The White House (2018b) *National Security Presidential Memorandum Regarding U.S. Conventional Arms Transfer Policy, Presidential Memorandum*. Washington, DC: The White House. Available at: www.whitehouse.gov/presi dential-actions/national-security-presidential-memorandum-regarding-u-s-con ventional-arms-transfer-policy/ (accessed: December 1, 2020).

Thompson, L. (2015) "Five reasons why Silicon Valley won't partner with the Pentagon," *Forbes*, April 27. Available at: www.forbes.com/sites/lor enthompson/2015/04/27/five-reasons-why-silicon-valley-wont-partner-with-the-pentagon/?sh=6afaedea4de9 (accessed: November 9, 2020).

Thompson, M. (2019) "The Incredibly Shrinking Defense Industry," *POGO*. Available at: www.pogo.org/analysis/2019/08/the-incredibly-shrinking-defense-industry/ (accessed: November 9, 2020).

Tirpak, J. A. (1998) "The distillation of the defense industry," *Air Force Magazine*, July 1. Available at: www.airforcemag.com/article/0798industry/ (accessed: November 7, 2020).

Tirpak, J. A. (2020) "Esper's approach to flat budgets mirrors USAF, keeps nukes a priority," *Air Force Magazine*, May 6. Available at: www.airforce mag.com/espers-approach-to-flat-budgets-mirrors-usaf-keeps-nukes-a-prior ity/ (accessed October 21, 2021).

TransDigm Incorporated (2017) *Onward & Upward. 2016 Annual Report.* Cleveland, OH: TransDigm. Available at: http://eproxymaterials.com/inter active/tdg2016/ (accessed: September 8, 2021).

Triezenberg, B. L., Steiner, C. P., Johnson, G., *et al.* (2020) *Assessing the Impact of U.S. Air Force National Security Space Launch Acquisition Decisions: An Independent Analysis of the Global Heavy Lift Launch Market.* Santa Monica, CA: RAND Corporation. doi: 10.7249/rr4251.

Trimble, S. (2019) "Competing proposals emerge as GBSD faces sole-source award decision," *Aviation Week*, August 2. Available at: https://aviationweek .com/missile-defense/competing-proposals-emerge-gbsd-faces-sole-source-award-decision (accessed: October 22, 2021).

Trimble, Steve, Lee Hudson and Michael Bruno (2019), Lockheed and the Pentagon Joust Over Lucrative F-35 Data Rights, Aviation Week, 25 November, p. 23.

TWI Global (2021) "What are Technology Readiness Levels (TRL)?" *TWI Global*. Available at: www.twi-global.com/technical-knowledge/faqs/tech nology-readiness-levels (accessed: February 25, 2021).

US Congress (2018) *H.R.5040 – 115th Congress (2017–2018): Export Control Reform Act of 2018.* Washington, DC: 115th Congress. Available at: www .congress.gov/bill/115th-congress/house-bill/5040 (accessed: December 1, 2020).

US Department of Defense (2011) *DOD News Briefing with Deputy Secretary Lynn and DOD Senior Leaders to Announce the Air Force KC-46A Tanker Contract Award.* Washington, DC: US Department of Defense. Available at: www.defense-aerospace.com/articles-view/verbatim/4/122913/media-con ference-on-usaf-tanker.html (accessed: December 2, 2020).

US Department of Defense (2018a) *Summary of the 2018 National Defense Strategy of the United States of America.* Washington, DC: US Department of Defense. Available at: https://dod.defense.gov/Portals/1/Documents/pubs/2018-National-Defense-Strategy-Summary.pdf (accessed: November 3, 2020).

US Department of Defense (2018b) *Fiscal Year 2017 Annual Industrial Capabilities Report to Congress.* Washington, DC: US Department of Defense. Available at: www.businessdefense.gov/Portals/51/Documents/ Resources/2017 AIC RTC 05–17–2018 – Public Release.pdf?ver=2018–05–17–224631–340 (accessed: December 3, 2020).

US Department of Defense (2019) *Fiscal Year 2018 Industrial Capabilities Annual Report to Congress.* Washington, DC: US Department of Defense. Available at: www.airforcemag.com/PDF/DocumentFile/Documents/2019/ DOD-Annual-Industrial-Capabilities-Report-to-Congress-for-FY-2018.pdf (accessed: December 3, 2020).

US Department of Defense (2020a) *Contracts for Aug. 7, 2020*. Washington, DC: US Department of Defense. Available at: www.defense.gov/Newsroom/Contracts/Contract/Article/2305454/ (accessed: November 9, 2020).

US Department of Defense (2020b) *Defense Acquisition System Directive Goes into Effect*. Washington, DC: US Department of Defense. Available at: www.defense.gov/Newsroom/Releases/Release/Article/2340746/defense-acquisition-system-directive-goes-into-effect/ (accessed: September 8, 2021).

US Department of Defense (2021) *Info Paper: Upcoming Jedi Cloud Litigation Milestone*, January 28. Washington, DC: US Department of Defense. Available at: www.nextgov.com/media/gbc/docs/pdfs_edit/ng_infopaper_jedi_litigation_01282012.pdf (accessed: September 8, 2021).

US Department of Defense Office of the Inspector General (2019) *Review of Parts Purchased from TransDigm Group, Inc. DODIG-2019–060*. Alexandria, VA: US Department of Defense Office of Inspector General. Available at: www.dodig.mil/reports.html/Article/1769041/review-of-parts-purchased-from-transdigm-group-inc-dodig-2019-060/ (accessed: November 9, 2020).

US Department of Defense Office of the Inspector General (2020) *Report on the Joint Enterprise Defense Infrastructure (JEDI) Cloud Procurement*. Alexandria, VA: US Department of Defense Office of Inspector General. Available at: https://media.defense.gov/2020/Apr/15/2002281438/-1/-1/1/report on the joint enterprise defense infrastructure (jedi) cloud procurement dodig-2020–079.pdf (accessed: December 2, 2020).

US Department of Health and Human Services (2020) *Trump Administration Uses Defense Production Act to Aid Our Most Vulnerable*. Washington, DC: US Department of Health and Human Services. Available at: www.hhs.gov/about/news/2020/08/20/trump-administration-uses-defense-production-act-to-aid-our-most-vulnerable.html (accessed: November 6, 2020).

US Department of the Treasury (2008) *CFIUS Reform: The Foreign Investment & National Security Act of 2007 (FINSA)*. Washington, DC: US Department of the Treasury. Available at: www.treasury.gov/resource-center/international/foreign-investment/Documents/Summary-FINSA.pdf (accessed: November 6, 2020).

US Department of the Treasury (2020) *The Committee on Foreign Investment in the United States (CFIUS)*. Washington, DC: US Department of the Treasury. Available at: https://home.treasury.gov/policy-issues/international/the-committee-on-foreign-investment-in-the-united-states-cfius (accessed: November 6, 2020).

US General Services Administration (2019) *Federal Acquisition Regulation (FAR)*. Washington, DC: US General Services Administration. Available at:

www.gsa.gov/policy-regulations/regulations/federal-acquisition-regulation-far (accessed: November 9, 2020).

US Government Accountability Office (2006), "Managing the Supplier Base in the 21st Century: Highlights of a GAO Forum, GAO 533-SP." Available at: www.gao.gov/new.items/d06533sp.pdf (accessed: September 8, 2021).

US Government Accountability Office (2007) *Defense Trade. Clarification and More Comprehensive Oversight of Export Exemptions Certified by DOD Are Needed.* Washington, DC: Government Accountability Office. Available at: www.gao.gov/assets/270/268269.pdf (accessed: December 1, 2020).

US Government Accountability Office (2015) *Evolved Expendable Launch Vehicle. The Air Force Needs to Adopt an Incremental Approach to Future Acquisition Planning to Enable Incorporation of Lessons Learned.* Washington, DC: US Government Accountability Office.

US Government Accountability Office (2016), Weapon System Requirements: Detailed Systems Engineering Prior to Product Development Positions Programs for Success, https://www.gao.gov/assets/gao-17-77.pdf

US Government Accountability Office (2017) *Solid Rocket Motors: DOD and Industry Are Addressing Challenges to Minimize Supply Concerns.* Washington, DC: US Government Accountability Office. Available at: www.gao.gov/assets/690/687977.pdf (accessed: December 7, 2020).

US Government Accountability Office (2018) *Buy American Act: Actions Needed to Improve Exception and Waiver Reporting and Selected Agency Guidance.* Washington, DC: US Government Accountability Office. Available at: www.gao.gov/assets/700/696086.pdf (accessed: November 5, 2020).

US Government Accountability Office (2019) *Weapons Systems Annual Assessment: Limited Use of Kowledge-Based Practices Continues to Undercut DOD's Investments.* Washington, DC: US Government Accountability Office. Available at: www.gao.gov/assets/700/698933.pdf (accessed: December 8, 2020).

US Office of Management and Budget (2020) *OMB Historical Tables 3.1.* Washington, DC: US Office of Management and Budget.

Wait, P. (2002) "Northrop Grumman creates two new sectors out of TRW, names leaders," *Washington Technology.* Available at: https://washingtontechnology.com/articles/2002/12/13/northrop-grumman-creates-two-new-sectors-out-of-trw-names-leaders.aspx (accessed: November 9, 2020).

Waldron, G. (2019) "K-FX CDR sets stage for prototype production," *Flight Global.* Available at: https://web.archive.org/web/20191120071732/ https://www.flightglobal.com/news/articles/k-fx-cdr-sets-stage-for-prototype-production-461123/ (accessed: September 8, 2021).

Warwick, G. (2016) "Assisting the human central to Pentagon's third offset," *Aviation Week*, January 18, p. 48. Available at: http://aviationweek.com/ defense/assisting-human-central-pentagon-s-third-offset (accessed: September 8, 2021).

Wayne, L.. (1998a) "The shrinking military complex; after the Cold War, the Pentagon is just another customer," *The New York Times*, February 27. Available at: www.nytimes.com/1998/02/27/business/shrinking-military-complex-after-cold-war-pentagon-just-another-customer.html (accessed: November 9, 2020).

Wayne, L. (1998b) "Lockheed cancels Northrop merger, citing U.S. stand," *The New York Times*, July 12. Available at: www.nytimes.com/1998/07/17/ business/lockheed-cancels-northrop-merger-citing-us-stand.html (accessed: November 7, 2020).

Wayne, L. (2006) "British arms merchant with passport to the Pentagon," *The New York Times*, August 16. Available at: www.nytimes.com/2006/08/16/busi ness/worldbusiness/16defense.html (accessed: September 8, 2021).

Weisgerber, M. (2019) "$85B nuclear missile competition gets messier as Feds investigate Northrop," *Defense One*. Available at: www.defenseone.com/ business/2019/10/usaf-puts-its-icbm-chips-northrop-feds-launch-investiga tion/160888/ (accessed: September 8, 2021).

Weisgerber, Marcus (2020) We Don't Have Enough Cash to Build New Nuclear Weapons, Says Air Force Chief, Defense One, https://www.defenseone.com/ politics/2020/07/we-dont-have-enough-cash-build-new-nuclear-weapons-says-air-force-chief/166598/

WikiMili (2020) "Tracor." Available at: https://wikimili.com/en/Tracor (accessed: September 8, 2021).

Wikipedia (2020) "Sanders Associates," last edited July 20. Available at: https://en. wikipedia.org/wiki/Sanders_Associates (accessed: September 8, 2021).

Wilkers, R. (2020) "Already two years behind schedule, JEDI fight to continue into 2021," *Washington Technology*. Available at: https://washingtontechnology.com/ articles/2020/09/16/jedi-case-whats-next.aspx (accessed: September 8, 2021).

Williamson, O. E. (1996) *The Mechanisms of Governance*. New York: Oxford University Press.

Wood, Dakota (2018), Rebuilding America's Military: Thinking About the Future, https://www.heritage.org/sites/default/files/2018-07/SR-203_web_0.pdf

Woolf, A. F. (2019) *U.S. Strategic Nuclear Forces: Background, Developments, and Issues*. Washington, DC: Congressional Research Service. Available at: www.everycrsreport.com/files/20190903_RL33640_608307c9acdc 9069c7dfcc02a5209304c5815d34.pdf (accessed: December 3, 2020).

WorldECR (2020) "US to ease export restrictions on armed drone exports," *WorldECR*. Available at: www.worldecr.com/news/us-to-ease-export-restric tions-on-armed-drone-exports/ (accessed: December 1, 2020).

Yoon-Hendricks, A. (2018) "Congress strengthens reviews of Chinese and other foreign investments," *The New York Times*, August 2. Available at: www.nytimes.com/2018/08/01/business/foreign-investment-united-states .html (accessed: November 6, 2020).

## Cambridge Elements ☰

# Defence Economics

### Keith Hartley
*University of York*

Keith Hartley was Professor of Economics and Director of the Centre for Defence Economics at the University of York, where he is now Emeritus Professor of Economics. He is the author of over 500 publications comprising journal articles, books and reports. His most recent books include *The Economics of Arms* (Agenda Publishing, 2017) and with Jean Belin (Eds) *The Economics of the Global Defence Industry* (Taylor and Francis, 2020). Hartley was founding Editor of the journal *Defence and Peace Economics*; a NATO Research Fellow; a QinetiQ Visiting Fellow; consultant to the UN, EC, EDA, UK MoD, HM Treasury, Trade and Industry, Business, Innovation and Skills and International Development and previously Special Adviser to the House of Commons Defence Committee.

### About the Series

Defence economics is a relatively new field within the discipline of economics. It studies all aspects of the economics of war and peace. It embraces a wide range of topics in both macroeconomics and microeconomics. *Cambridge Elements in Defence Economics* aims to publish original and authoritative papers in the field. These include expert surveys of the foundations of the discipline, its historical development and contributions developing new and novel topics. They are valuable contributions to both research and teaching in universities and colleges, and also appeal to other specialist groups comprising politicians, military and industrial personnel as well as informed general readers.

# Cambridge Elements ≡

# Defence Economics

---

## Elements in the Series

Printed in the United States
by Baker & Taylor Publisher Services